Social Adjustment and Personality Development in Children

SOCIAL ADJUSTMENT AND PERSONALITY DEVELOPMENT IN CHILDREN

Merrill Roff

S. B. Sells

Mary M. Golden

THE UNIVERSITY OF MINNESOTA
PRESS • MINNEAPOLIS

Library of Congress Catalog Card Number: 72-79100

ISBN 0-8166-0660-9

Preface

American society is said to be highly status conscious, and this is apparent in the emphasis on status in most areas of interpersonal interaction. Among the most interesting and illuminating phenomena of social interaction are the patterns, bases, and consequences of social acceptance and rejection in the peer society of children. The studies which comprise the research basis for this book have demonstrated that peer relations, even among young children, follow lawful, predictable patterns. Popularity with peers is no superficial or casual matter. Many variables, rooted deeply in individual life situations and backgrounds, moderate experience and affect the attractiveness of the child to his school- and age-mates as well as his developing attitudes and personality. The interplay of social and developmental processes is beautifully illustrated in these studies.

The influence of childhood peer relations in personality development reflects the importance of peer society in the elementary school years. Peer acceptance implies not only popularity, but also deference and esteem and is a coveted status, awarded disproportionately to those perceived as brighter, better endowed socially as well as biologically, better situated in the social hierarchy, and more fortunate in respect to family position and possessions. Peer rejection is more often the lot of the less fortunate, the less able, the less effective, and the socially less advantaged. Developing children react to acceptance or rejection in a way that affects their self-concepts and their attitudes toward others. The result is apparently a learning process which resembles the sociologists' "self-fulfilling prophecy." Acceptance is followed by self-esteem and outgoing, accepting attitudes toward others, which in turn invites greater acceptance. On the other hand, rejection is associated with self-devaluation and hostile attitudes, which invite further rejection.

In the studies reported here, acceptance and rejection by peers were measured by peer ratings of like-sex classmates in nineteen cities in Texas and two large cities in Minnesota. An initial sample of about 38,000 children of both sexes was studied in the basic, first-year investigation. Follow-up studies of smaller groups were carried out in four succeeding years. These studies investigated the characteristics of the peer-rating measures as well as their relations to family background factors, measures of intelligence, birth order, ethnic group membership, school grades, and a number of aspects of the developing personality — health, self-concept, personality traits. In addition to retrospective linkages of peer status with background and individual characteristics, two major studies were carried out in a predictive framework, which related peer status in the early grades to subsequent early delinquency and school dropout.

Peer acceptance was found to be positively associated with higher socioeconomic status, higher intelligence, higher educational level of parents, loving and casual parental attitudes, better health, and a number of other positive background factors; the converse was found for peer rejection. The influence of family-associated factors was clearly demonstrated by comparison of peer ratings of siblings and twins with those of randomly assembled sets of children.

The predictive study of early delinquency was especially interesting because it demonstrated not only a significant association with peer status, but also a tendency for different effects at upper and lower socioeconomic levels. At the lower levels, where certain behaviors considered delinquent by the middle class tend to be generally accepted, children of high peer status were often found to be delinquent. This reflects the fact that, in the lower strata, popularity and leadership are associated with behavior which, though socially unacceptable to the middle class, is acceptable and admired in the adult and peer society of those strata.

The overall implications of this book require serious study. Apart from the light that the book sheds on the strategic, pivotal importance of peer relations in childhood, it raises sober questions concerning the feasibility of individual intervention measures that seem to by-pass the competitive social inequities that underlie the phenomena associated with acceptance and rejection. Children fortunate enough to be born in middle- and upper-class families, with educated, loving parents appear to have many favorable influences operating in their personality development. On the other hand, the less fortunate seem to be destined to suffer the effects of the unfavorable influences described in this book. The challenge is almost overwhelming to achieve favorable effects in individual development in the context of the social forces implied.

M. R.
S. B. S.
M. M. G.

Minneapolis
November 1971

Table of Contents

Social Adjustment and Personality Development in Children

1

~~~~~

Introduction

This book describes a five-year program of research on the social adjustment of schoolchildren in the third through the sixth grades. The entire sample, including all those for whom some information was available, contained some 40,000 children, about equally divided between Texas and Minnesota. Smaller subsamples (about 5,000 pupils) were used for a four-year longitudinal study. The many correlates of social adjustment were studied with subsamples of various kinds. The measures of social adjustment used were, first, peer acceptance-rejection scores obtained from pupils' choices of classmates and, second, teachers' ratings of the peer status of children in their classes.

This large-scale study of peer status during childhood was suggested by the results of earlier research by Roff (1956, 1957, 1959, 1960, 1961, 1963, 1965, 1966) on the adult adjustment of persons who as boys had been dealt with in child guidance clinics. Using adult information obtained from the records of the military services and related organizations, it was found that poor peer adjustment during childhood was predictive of a variety of adult maladjustments (neuroses, schizophrenia, severe bad conduct problems, homosexuality, schizoid personality, and other personality disorders). Cases from clinics located in several major cities of the country were followed up so that the total sample size was large enough to yield stable results, even for maladjustments of rather infrequent occurrence.

These earlier studies had several limitations: samples obtained

3

from child guidance clinics are not representative of the general populations of the cities in which they are located; work was done only with male subjects because of the nature of the criterion information; and the information on peer adjustment contained in the clinic records consisted primarily of teachers' observations. It therefore seemed desirable to get peer status measures based on choices made by the children themselves for total school populations. This would both quantify the assessment of peer acceptance-rejection and give samples of the entire public school population for the grades included in most of the cities being studied.

It was decided to carry out the study simultaneously on samples of the school populations of Texas and Minnesota. Samples of large size were planned to assure adequate numbers when broken down by school grade, sex, socioeconomic level, ethnic group, and other relevant bases of classification, and to permit the comparison of subgroups based on one or another of these factors. If it is assumed that thorough cross-validation requires a completely new and independent sample, influenced by factors different from those of the sample on which initial results were found, rather than additional cases drawn essentially from the same original sample source, the choice of two widely separated geographic areas, differing in ethnic, socioeconomic, and cultural backgrounds was indicated. No examples have been found of large-scale studies of this kind which applied the same procedures to samples from differently constituted populations. Finally, by avoiding the difficulties and delays usually involved in adequate replication, the simultaneous testing program in the two different states assured replication without loss of valuable time. It is recognized, in textbook discussions of statistical inference, that the commonly used sampling error procedures are strictly applicable only when going from one randomly selected sample to another drawn from the same parent population. In actual practice, it is common for psychologists to attach error values to their statistical results, and then to use these as a license for extending the results to populations altogether different from their sample's parent population. This is particularly characteristic of experimental psychology, where there are those who have no hesitation in assuming that results obtained on one species may be considered applicable to quite different species. Because two somewhat different populations were involved, it was decided to rely throughout this book much more on cross-replication and subgroup cross-validation than on conventional statistical error values. There was occasionally a convergence of values which was striking with sample sizes as large as those studied here. Under some other circumstances the results diverged in the two states. The customary procedures of statistical inference were not applicable, since the two base populations were demonstrably different in certain respects. The term *cross-population robustness* has been used to refer to concordant results from different base populations (Roff, 1970).

In the initial, first-year administration, some information on peer status was obtained for about 38,000 boys and girls in grades three through six in nineteen cities in Texas and two large cities in Minnesota. Complete data for the first-year study was available for 34,366 subjects. When new pupils moving into the study over the next four years are included, the total sample for which some information was obtained exceeds 40,000. A longitudinal study was continued for four successive years based on smaller samples of children in each state.

The long-term project plan was to obtain various types of follow-up information at later ages, extending into the adult period, for children from these samples. The present book gives longitudinal information over a four-year period, and demonstrates a relationship between peer scores and the real life adjustment criterion of early juvenile delinquency. Some promising preliminary results were also obtained for predicting a second real life criterion, dropping out of school; presentation of these results will await the completion of studies of larger, more comprehensive samples, when formal education has been completed.

The plan of the book may be outlined briefly to indicate the kinds of information it contains. Chapter 2, on procedures and samples, gives a detailed description of what was done, and why, in obtaining and analyzing the peer choices of this very large total sample. The study was designed so that the peer choices could be expressed on IBM cards which could be fed directly into a computer system. Only with a data analysis procedure of this kind could such a large quantity of material have been handled at a moderate cost. The latter part of the chapter draws from the large number of qualitative descriptions by school personnel, obtained in the course of the study, to illustrate the personality characteristics and life situations of boys and girls varying in score level and in various other respects.

This is followed by a chapter giving statistical information on the reliability and intercorrelations of the different scores obtained. A comprehensive presentation is also given of data indicating stability and change in the peer status scores through the period of this part of the study.

The correlations that indicate the level of accuracy of teachers' ratings when compared with the peer choices made by children are given in detail. The validity of teacher ratings is important, because the collection of these entails less difficulty than obtaining children's peer choices, particularly the negative ones. Some parents objected to the peer choice procedure, and particularly to the use of negative choices, on the ethical ground that they try to teach their children to like everyone just the same. This teaching was obviously not completely successful, since in all classes some children were better liked than others. The qualitative protocols indicate clearly that situations involving choosing are a normal part of many school settings. These were full of statements such as "she is usually one of the first ones chosen for any activity" or "he is almost always the last one chosen." When the teacher is acquainted with her class, her ratings will show a substantial correlation with pupil choices. They can be used as an approximate substitute for negative peer choices.

The data obtained also provide information on several other problems which have received much discussion over the years. One of these is the relationship between teachers' social class background and their ability to understand children of social class different from their own. Insofar as accuracy of teacher ratings of the peer status of their children is an indication of their understanding of their pupils, there was no marked difference in the correlations between teacher ratings and acceptance-rejection scores at different socioeconomic levels. These samples showed little evidence of the widely heralded gap between the middle-class teacher and the lower-class child.

Another problem that has received a good deal of attention is that of differences between teachers in their ability to judge accurately the peer status of their pupils. Because of our longitudinal design, it was possible to compare the rating accuracy of a set of teachers in successive years, when they had different classes. It was found that the differences in the pupils making up particular classes tended to outweigh any ability to judge people as a trait of the individual teachers. Some classes can be rated more accurately than others.

A problem which has received substantial attention in earlier research work on "social perception" is the relation between the peer status of persons making choices and that of persons they choose. This problem is explored with much larger samples than have ever been used before, with results of unusual stability. With large samples from both states, reliable and accurately replicated results indicated that the choice status of chooser and chosen are essentially unrelated, the correlations for positive choices being near zero and those for negative choices not exceeding .19. These results are highly relevant to research in sociometry and interpersonal perception. Despite the claims of numerous writers that matrix methods are necessary in computing scores in order to represent the status of choosers in computing the status of individuals chosen, little empirical work has appeared in support of their arguments. The results of this study, and the agreement between the two state samples, indicate that the matrix approach is unnecessary.

In discussions of the relations between family characteristics and the personalities of children, the implicit assumption is too frequently made that a given set of family characteristics will produce a single type of outcome in children. This is, of course, not true, since brothers differ from one another and sisters differ from one another. Our large samples in the two states provided a unique opportunity to explore twin and sibling resemblances in peer status. The degree of resemblance and difference is presented in detail. Using intraclass correlation to assess resemblance within family groups and control groups of unrelated children, a continuum of increasing resemblance was found, ranging from correlations of zero for controls, up to .38 for siblings, and up to .80 for identical twins. Within sibling and fraternal twin groups, like-sex members were more highly similar in peer scores than unlike-sex members.

It has long been known that there is a relation between intelligence and choice status in children. This relation can be analyzed in more detail by asking whether the relationship would be similar or different at different levels of the socioeconomic scale. Evidence is presented that the relationship between intelligence and peer status is about the same at different socioeconomic levels, and for boys and girls.

A second family variable which has attracted attention for a long time is that of birth order. In line with most other studies, it was found that the effects of birth order, though detectable, are too small to be of much importance.

The relation between racial or ethnic background and the characteristics of children is of great interest at the present time. The situation of black pupils was markedly different in the two states. In Texas the blacks were in segregated schools at the time the study was carried out. In Minnesota, on the other hand, there was no legal segregation, but there was some segregation by neighborhood. By Minnesota law, there is no official record of the race of pupils. All of these factors operated to limit markedly the information obtainable about the effects of race on peer status in racially mixed groups. On the other hand, in both states it was possible to compare peer status of a distinct ethnic group consisting of those with Spanish surnames with that of a control group drawn from the same classes. A small difference in favor of the control group was found on one measure in Texas, but not in Minnesota.

It is not possible to make anything approaching a systematic study of the families of 40,000 pupils. Some family information was obtained from school personnel for selected high and low choice pupils. In addition, intensive study was made of approximately 100 families in one Texas city. All this information agrees in indicating the importance of the family as an influence on the peer status of the children. Peer scores were shown to be significantly correlated with socioeconomic status (SES), birth order, and a number of indices of family pathology, relating to poverty, ignorance, indigence, and family disorganization.

The full-scale follow-up of these children has not yet been made. Information was available, however, during the period of this study concerning early juvenile delinquency and dropping out of school. Our predictions with relation to juvenile delinquency were in large part confirmed, but an unexpected finding there made this one of the most interesting sets of data in the entire study.

From the viewpoint of child development, it appears that parents of higher SES, who tend to raise their children in more abundant and enlightened home environments, and who are less prone to tension due to deprivation, illness, or interpersonal conflict, are more likely to acquire and project loving and flexible attitudes toward their children. Such a comfortable, enlightened, and ego-satisfying background tends to produce healthy, bright, and outgoing children, with high self-esteem, who accept and in turn are accepted by peers. In relation to subsequent life experience, such children are more likely to approach maturity without undue strain and to adjust well in school and society. At the opposite pole, poverty, discontent, ignorance, and frustration at the parental level tend to produce rejecting and demanding parents, who in turn raise children poor in health, intelligence, and self-esteem, who project attitudes of hostility to others and in turn are rejected. Such children are vulnerable to the same problems that defeated their parents and are more likely to develop into maladjusted youth and adults.

Peer rejection, which has been shown elsewhere (Roff, 1957, 1960, 1961, 1963, 1965) to be a precursor of later severe maladjustment, is not an isolated event randomly distributed among the child population. The results reported here tie it to social forces of considerable generality and of major significance. It appears that child-oriented programs of enriched educational offerings and group activities, which enjoy current popularity among agencies concerned with underprivileged, disadvantaged, maladjusted, and delinquent youth, are focused on symptoms rather than causes. Such approaches may have short-term value as palliative measures, but the indications of the present research suggest that their principal value may be only to buy time until more fundamental measures, designed to attack the roots of the problems, can be put into effective operation.

Prescription of such measures is beyond the scope of this report and beyond the capability of its authors. Indeed, there are many loose ends in the research data, mentioned throughout the report, which require further study. These include more extensive investigation of the ethnic and racial minorities in the samples, and extension of the follow-up studies in relation to delinquency and dropping out of school. The whole area of adult adjustments has yet to be explored.

No research is ever complete. However, it is hoped that in this report there will be found a synthesis of principles that have appeared segmentally in the literature and a marshalling of evidence concerning the antecedents and consequences of peer acceptance-rejection that may stimulate both research and administrative interest in this area of human behavior.

2

※※※※

Procedures,
Samples, and Scores

Detailed information on peer acceptance-rejection is not ordinarily found in school records, except perhaps for the small minority who are referred for psychological services. In planning data collection, four possible approaches were considered: observation, self-report, peer nominations, and teacher ratings. Observation reports, which describe actual instances of leadership and rejection in the classroom and on the playground, might have been obtained through teachers or project staff members. However, this would have been expensive. It would have run the risk of disturbing the "natural" social situation by the presence of strangers. It would still need to be quantified even when adequately recorded and — perhaps most importantly — would be an inadequate way of describing children who were neither outstanding leaders nor actively rejected. Self-report instruments, in which each student attempts to assess his own peer status, are of uncertain validity (Kogan & Tagiuri, 1958; Satterlee, 1955) and might increase objections from school personnel and parents. They were judged to be somewhat unsatisfactory for large-scale application, but were used in a special study of a relatively small sample, for purposes of comparison with other procedures (see pp. 139–140 below).

The peer choice method in which pupils indicate those in the same class whom they like most and like least gives a direct method of measuring peer status. This procedure yields numerical scores for the Like Most (LM) and Like Least (LL) choices received by each child, and with very little further effort gives a combination score consisting of the number of Like Most minus the number of Like Least (LM – LL) votes received. These scores give a continuum of acceptance-rejection which shows each child's place with respect to his classmates. Teacher ratings, in which teachers judge the peer status of boys and girls in their classes, have been shown to be substantially, though no means perfectly, correlated with peer choice scores. The most important requirement for getting adequate teacher ratings is that the teacher should have been associated with the pupils long enough to know them well.

Since it seemed desirable to compare the results of positive and negative peer choices and Teacher Ratings with each other and with other kinds of current and follow-up information, it was decided to obtain both peer choices and Teacher Ratings for all pupils. It was practicable to obtain both at approximately the same period of time, although the Teacher Ratings had to be made and collected before the administration of the peer choice procedure so that teachers would not be influenced in their rating by results of the peer nominations. For the large-scale survey planned, the methods used had to meet the criteria of economy, ease of handling, and adaptability to an automatic data processing system. Because it is printed to facilitate correct marking and provides enough spaces so that ratings could be obtained on a single card, the IBM Mark Sense card seemed ideally suited to the present study, although more efficient optical scanning equipment has become commercially available since the study was planned. Once the peer nominations and the Teacher Ratings were marked on their respective cards, these could be punched mechanically without the use of key-punch operators; all subsequent counts, transformations, correlations, and other analyses could be performed at high speed on automatic card machines and computers.

PEER CHOICE MEASURES

Based on the Mark Sense equipment (see Appendix A), a choice procedure was designed involving the following features.

a. Peer choices and teacher ratings were made directly on Mark Sense cards specially designed for this study using mimeographed class rosters with identification numbers corresponding to card columns. Separate rosters were prepared for boys and for girls, and choices were made only within the same sex. Each child in the class was listed on the appropriate roster with an identification number. Choices were made by simply marking the numbers of the children chosen in the spaces provided for Like Most and Like Least.

b. Pretests indicated that group administration of peer nominations was easily possible for third-graders. Subsequent data analyses showed that the third-graders responded as well as older children did.

c. Lists of boy and girl class members were obtained from the teachers a week or so before the administration dates. This permitted the duplication of these lists so that each child would have his own copy to use in making his choices. These rosters included dates of birth in order to facilitate identification and to give a record of ages.

d. Rating procedures were administered by the classroom teachers and returned to the project staff by school coordinators. All Teacher Ratings (TR) were collected before the peer choice administration.

e. Peer choices were made separately by sex group: boys rated only boys, and girls only girls. This procedure was adopted after consideration of the social relations between boys and girls in these grades — it seemed that whether a child gets along well with others of the same sex is of primary interest at this age level. Roster lists and nominating cards for boys and girls were of different colors to eliminate confusion during administration and to assist in keeping the two sets of data separate.

f. Peer choices were restricted to those individuals on the lists furnished. Choices of pupils in other classes were not permitted. In class-groups of nine or more, pupils were instructed to make four LM choices and two LL choices. Appropriate reductions in numbers chosen were made for class-groups of smaller size.

Selection of Rating Dimensions. The selection of Like Most and Like Least as the dimensions on which the ratings were to be made was influenced partly by the fact that these general phrases were close to the original findings of the relations between childhood peer status and adult maladjustment by Roff (1956, 1957, 1959, 1960, 1961, 1963, 1965, 1966). It was also based on a review of the literature and some pretesting. The results of various questions such as "Who is your best friend?" and "With whom do you like to study?" are ordinarily highly intercorrelated. We decided that the direct questions of LM and LL

13

were most clearly related to our research problems and involved the fewest semantic assumptions.

Inclusion of "Negative" Ratings. It is generally known by researchers who have used choice procedures that the negative nomination presents a rather severe problem. Many people of all ages resist making derogatory or even mildly negative statements about their fellows. Personality research is currently a controversial issue in American schools, and objections have occasionally been aroused by the inclusion of the negative ratings. Nevertheless, both the literature (Gronlund, 1959; Justman & Wrightstone, 1951) and the pretest results showed clearly that the choice status of children might vary considerably on LM and LL ratings, and that LL was not a highly predictable opposite of LM. The median correlation between the two is about .50. Although a large number of LL votes could be accepted as an indicator of rejection by peers, lack of LM votes may not indicate the same status. Rather, the latter may merely reflect the nonselection of uninteresting or newly arrived individuals who are not disliked, and thus are not chosen as negative choices. For these reasons, and because Roff's prior studies have emphasized the importance of the liked-least as well as the liked-most end of the acceptance-rejection continuum, it was decided to include the LL ratings.

The decision to obtain four LM ratings and only two LL ratings for average or large-sized classes was a move toward decreasing antipathy toward the negative ratings. This was made after much discussion and search for a means of making the negative rating as palatable as possible without destroying its validity. Choice of the term *like least* rather than *dislike* reflected the same thinking. In discussing the project with school officials, PTA representatives, and teachers, it was apparent that *like least* seemed more acceptable and less likely to be considered contrary to religious or ethical principles, whereas *dislike* would be considered objectionable by some people.

Scores Derived. Rating cards were punched from the Mark Sense cards, using the IBM 514 Reproducing Punch. These were then run through an IBM 1620 computer which counted the number of LM and LL votes received by each member of each class-group. Standard scores (z scores) were then computed not only for the LM and LL choices but also for the composite LM – LL. The LL scores were reflected so that a high number of choices was always at the low end. Based on subsequent experience, a second composite score was later computed and converted to z-score form. This was a combined LM − LL score and TR score, with the peer choice composite given a weight of two and the TR scores a weight of one — that is, $2(LM - LL) + TR$. The z scores, which were computed with a mean of five and a standard deviation of one, were adopted as a means of correcting for variations in class size. Thus, the scores reflected deviation from class means in units of standard deviations rather than absolute number of votes received, which could vary markedly on the basis of group size without giving an accurate indication of sociometric status. The use of five as the mean rather than zero eliminated negative scores and simplified computation.

The Mark Sense procedure worked almost perfectly throughout the study. Although the cards had to be visually inspected to remove superfluous marks from the electrographic pencils, the processing of cards through the reproducer and computer replaced the prohibitive task of manual counting with an almost effortless, but vastly more accurate machine process. The tabulations of votes and computation of scores were accomplished rapidly, accurately, and economically. (Appendix A presents specimen forms and instructions.)

TEACHER RATINGS

Teacher Ratings were completed before the peer nomination procedure was administered to assure that the ratings were made before teachers saw the results of the peer choices. In the first year of the study, the TR procedure employed a four-step scale, by means of which each teacher made a judgment about the peer relations of each pupil in his or her class as follows: (1) exceptionally good peer relations; (2) average — no negative indications or outstanding positive indications; (3) borderline rejection; (4) clearly rejected by peers.

Inspection of the descriptions of first-year ratings indicated a need for extension of the scale since there was an excess of ratings of 2, and the rating of 4 was rarely used. The TR scale was carefully revised, using descriptive information obtained during the first year, into a 7-point scale which contained more specific descriptions at various scale points than the scale used earlier. A copy of this is given in Appendix A. The seven points of this scale, which was used for the remainder of the study, are as follows: (1) extremely high — outstanding peer relations; (2) extremely high — superior peer relations; (3) high acceptance among peers; (4) moderate acceptance among peers; (5) low peer relations; (6) rejected generally by peers; (7) rejected entirely by peers.

Teacher rating scales were color-coded for boys and girls. Programs for converting TR to z scores, coordinated with those for converting peer nominations, were developed. This integrated program proved to be rapid and efficient.

Interview Material from School Personnel. In order to obtain detailed qualitative information about some of the children, in addition to the quantitative peer scores and teacher ratings, arrangements were made to obtain descriptions of children from the Minnesota sample. Information was obtained from the classroom teachers who were familiar with the children described through having them in class throughout the school day. Earlier work with child guidance clinic case histories had led to a strong appreciation of the value of careful qualitative descriptions of children made by professionally trained persons who know them well.

Since it was not feasible to conduct interviews for all the children in the Minnesota sample, it was decided to obtain interviews on between 10 and 15 per cent of the children. Interviews were obtained for approximately 1,232 boys and 1,232 girls from the Minnesota sample. The sample was constructed on the basis of the peer status scores of the children in the class. It included four children per class: the lowest boy and the lowest girl, in terms of standard scores, the highest boy or girl, and a middle pupil opposite in sex to the highest boy or girl. This gave a sample with an equal number of boys and girls, half with the lowest peer status in their classes, and the other half approximately equally divided between high and middle status.

The interviews were conducted by the visiting teachers at each school, who were paid for the work which they completed during their free time. They followed a structured interview outline, which was prepared with the assistance of school personnel. The interviewers tape-recorded the interview information immediately following the interview, and the tapes were later transcribed by project personnel. The interview outline included four areas, as indicated below. These were covered systematically in each interview, in the order listed.

I. Personal Characteristics of the Child
   1. Describe the child's physical appearance.
   2. What individualizes this child? How is he like or different from other children?
   3. What are his particular strengths or weaknesses?

II. Child's Behavior
   1. Describe this child's behavior on the playground.
   2. Describe this child's behavior in the classroom and in the building.
   3. Describe this child's behavior in relation to other students.
   4. Describe this child's behavior in relation to this teacher.
   5. Have you noticed any significant change in his behavior this year?

III. Classmates' Reactions
   1. What do you consider to be typical reactions of the other students toward this child?
   2. What does he (or she) do to cause these reactions in the other children?

IV. Family
   1. What do you see as significant strengths and weaknesses present in this family?

Sample descriptions obtained in this interview are shown in Chapters 2, 5, and 8. These have proved indispensable in making interpretations of some of the quantitative findings.

In Texas, instead of the interview procedure, a Teachers Comment Form was used for all students who received the lowest teacher ratings. These were also very useful in giving a picture of the characteristics of the least-liked boys and girls.

OTHER INFORMATION

In addition to the information obtained from the teacher interview material, information on family background, IQ, birth order, sex of siblings, socioeconomic level of the school and the family, and school achievement was obtained for various subsamples for analysis in connection with peer acceptance-rejection.

Socioeconomic Status. In the Minnesota part of the study, the different schools were grouped into quartiles based on the SES of the area in which they were located, and these quartiles were regularly treated as separate subsamples, comparable to the different cities in the Texas sample. There are many variations in detail possible in defining SES, but the end results tend to be very highly correlated with one another. In the present study, socioeconomic level was determined on a census tract basis, making use of a combination of adult income and education from the 1960 census values (U.S. Bureau of the Census, 1962). Separate classification of census tracts on these two criteria gave highly similar results. In a second census report (1963) which presents scores based on these two variables for different occupations, it was observed that "Consideration was given to the differential weighting of the component items in arriving at a socioeconomic score. The decision was made instead to use a simple average of the component scores, largely because no adequate bases for determining weights were established." We had already reached the same conclusion, and done the same thing.

Other information indicates that this classification of schools would correspond closely to that made by any other relevant index of SES, of which there are many. The difference in IQ points between the upper and lower socioeconomic levels on the Lorge-Thorndike test was approximately the same as the difference between high and low socioeconomic levels of the Stanford-Binet, when these were classified according to occupational level of father (McNemar, 1942). The differences found here are greater than those reported by Anderson (1962) for the Lorge-Thorndike test for a partial sample from Syracuse, New York; he estimated SES on the basis of the Sims Social Class Identification Scale.

By our procedure, SES is treated as a continuous variable which could as well be divided into fifths, sixths, sevenths, and so forth, or, as is done at one point in this study (see p. 151), into eighths. These divisions do not correspond to such discrete "classes" as those sometimes referred to as "upper-middle," or "lower-lower." The loss in familiarity to some readers should be compensated for by the fact that quartiles or other similar subdivisions indicate the proportion of the total sample that they include.

Follow-Up Studies: Later Correlates of Peer Acceptance-Rejection. Repeated administration of the peer choice procedures over a four-year period accumulated year-to-year scores for almost 5,000 pupils. This made it possible to relate scores obtained in one year to those obtained in subsequent years, and thus to gain information about stability and change in status throughout the grade school period in Minnesota and into the junior high school period in Texas. Because of the relatively large size of junior high schools in the two Minnesota cities, no attempt was made to administer the peer choice procedure after the sixth grade. In some smaller Texas cities it was found to be practical to continue the administration into junior high school. The results of this will be presented in Chapter 3.

It was expected that even during the relatively short follow-up period of four years it would be possible to find real life criteria of adjustment or maladjustment with which the peer scores could be compared. In Minnesota, juvenile court files were checked to determine which children from our sample had been apprehended as early juvenile delinquents, and in Texas the names of children who had dropped out of school were obtained. Results of studies using this information are presented in Chapter 8. More extensive and detailed follow-up studies will be possible as the sample matures.

Family Factors Associated with Peer Acceptance-Rejection. Information about family factors related to peer status was obtained in various ways. Part of the Minnesota interview was devoted to family information, but this was sometimes rather sparse, due to lack of contact between the school and the family. In Texas, information concerning family adjustment was obtained for the families of 685 pupils. The results of studies of the relations between family factors and peer status are presented in Chapter 6. A more intensive analysis of volunteer families of 97 pupils from the study sample was conducted by Samuel Cox. Measures of attitude concerning child-bearing as well as extensive information on socioeconomic status and family problems were obtained from the parents and children involved. Personality and health information about the child was also obtained. A condensed summary of this study appears in Chapter 7.

SAMPLING DESIGN

An overall picture of the sample, year by year, is given in Table 1. Of the nineteen Texas school districts participating in the first year, results for all four years were obtained in four cities. One of the two Minnesota cities participated for four years. In the other, during the fourth year, instead of re-administering, the teacher interviews only were obtained for all those still in the city for whom interviews had

Table 1. Total Samples for the Four Years of the Study,
Year to Year and Longitudinal

State and Year of Study	No. of Districts	No. of Pupils[a]
Total Sample		
First year		
Texas	19	17,291
Minnesota	2	17,075
Total	21	34,366
Second year		
Texas	10	8,482
Minnesota	1	4,715
Total	11	13,197
Third year		
Texas	5	3,721
Minnesota	1	3,080
Total	6	6,801
Fourth year		
Texas	4	2,633
Minnesota	1	2,307
Total	5	4,940
Longitudinal Sample		
First and second years		
Texas		6,518 (5,518)
Minnesota		2,944
Total		9,462
First, second, and third years		
Texas		2,257 (1,419)
Minnesota		1,620
Total		3,877
First, second, third, and fourth years		
Texas		1,307 (486)
Minnesota		670[b]
Total		1,977

[a]Texas included junior high students; number of grade school children is in parentheses.

[b]The longitudinal study in Minnesota included one fewer school grade in each successive year. The four-year longitudinal sample includes only those who were in the third grade in one city during the first administration.

originally been obtained. The number of schools, classes, teachers, and pupils in the continuing cities varied somewhat from year to year. As a result, each year there were some cases lost and some added, as well as a large number of continuing pupils. For some analyses, the total-year samples were used; for others, such as year-to-year correlational studies, it was necessary to match names and include only the continuing (longitudinal) sample.

Table 1 shows the total sample for whom complete information was obtained in the four consecutive years. It should be remembered that with each subsequent year, there was one fewer school grade in the sample — that is, in the first year we had grades three through six, in the second year grades four through six, and so on. In Texas, testing was continued through junior high school, but the samples studied were not so large as those in the grade school period. The longitudinal sample is also shown, year by year. These are the pupils for whom complete information was available for the years listed, so that the four-year sample would include all those for whom we had complete information for all four years.

Details of Sampling Procedure. Classroom samples were determined by the registration as of the day on which the peer choices were made. Teachers added or deleted names reflecting changes in class membership in the week or so since they had provided the rosters. Absent pupils were rated by their class groups. Teachers were not instructed to obtain peer choices later from absentees although some teachers undoubtedly did this before returning the cards.

SCORE DISTRIBUTIONS AND RELIABILITIES

Both the peer choices and the teacher ratings were put into standard score (z score) form, to compensate for differences in class size, and to facilitate their manipulation and comprehension over a large number of classes. The z-score distributions (with a mean of 5.0 and a standard deviation of 1.0) are shown in Table 2. The differences in distributions between Texas and Minnesota were negligible. (LL scores were reflected in sign so that no LL choices received the highest z score, to afford consistent interpretation of all peer score measures.) TR's on the four- and seven-point scales are listed separately. While peer choices were made within class-groups of like sex, TR were made for the entire class by one rater. Thus, while the mean and standard deviation of TR are 5.0 and 1.0, respectively, for the distribution of boys and girls combined, the mean TR for girls tends to be slightly higher than that for boys. Texas and Minnesota peer choice scores are distributed nearly identically, but this agreement did not hold for the TR. In view of similarity of the peer choice distributions, it is apparent that the Texas and Minnesota teachers used different subjective judgment scales. The Texas teachers reported relatively less maladjustment in peer relations than did the Minnesota teachers.

Table 2. Percentage of Peer Rating Scores in Each z-Score Interval for First-Year Samples, Texas and Minnesota Combined

z-Score Interval	LM	LL	LM – LL	TR (4 point)	TR (7 point)
7.0 and above	3.6		1.1	.2	1.1
6.5–6.9	6.3	.2	4.9	2.4	5.0
6.0–6.4	9.1	7.0	11.0	15.8	7.8
5.5–5.9	11.3	34.4	16.4	7.6	14.9
5.0–5.4	17.1	24.8	22.1	25.5	18.2
4.5–4.9	17.0	11.1	17.8	18.3	28.9
4.0–4.4	24.1	7.6	12.5	9.0	14.3
3.5–3.9	10.4	5.3	7.4	6.8	7.2
3.0–3.4	1.1	3.9	4.3	3.0	2.2
2.5–2.9		3.5	2.1	1.1	.4
2.0–2.4		1.5	.4	.3	
Below 2.0		.7			
Total	100.0	100.0	100.0	100.0	100.0

A graphic picture of the distribution for LM, LL, and LM – LL for the total population at the time of first testing is shown in Figure 1. It can be seen that the LM and LL scores are markedly skewed, whereas the LM – LL scores have a relatively symmetrical distribution. The TR distribution on the 4-point scale is skewed toward the negative extreme and tends toward biomodality; the distribution on the 7-point scale is smoother and more nearly symmetrical.

Split-Half Reliabilities. The use of reliability procedures which have been developed for mental tests has received considerable discussion in the sociometric literature (Gronlund, 1959). The split-half method gives information only about the agreement of other members of the immediate group at a particular moment. It does not tell what a child's score would be in a somewhat differently constituted group. Possibly his score would be somewhat higher or lower if he happened

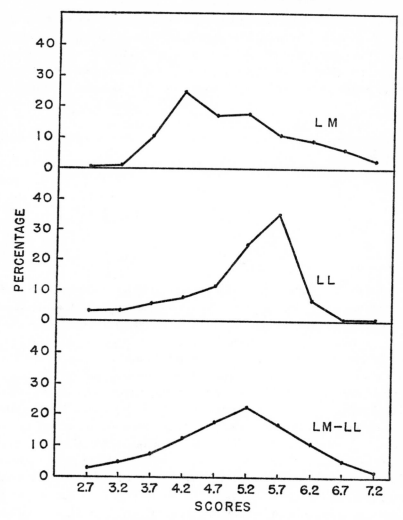

Figure 1. Distributions of Like Most (LM), Like Least (LL), and Like Most minus Like Least scores for total first-year sample. The curve for LL has been reversed so that a high number of choices is at the left end.

to be in a different class. Some change of pupils occurs from year to year, and this pupil shift contributes to the size of the year-to-year correlations.

These split-half correlations were obtained by correlating each child's nomination by one-half of the same-sex members of the class with these nominations by the other half, then correcting the correlation by the conventional application of the double length formula. The results obtained in this way are presented in various breakdowns. Table 3 compares reliability coefficients for the first-year administra-

Table 3. Mean Split-Half Reliability Coefficients for LM and LL
First-Year Scores by State, Grade, and Sex

Grade and Sex	LM		LL	
	Minnesota[a]	Texas[b]	Minnesota[a]	Texas[b]
Third	.67	.69	.63	.65
Fourth	.67	.69	.70	.74
Fifth	.66	.71	.74	.75
Sixth	.61	.71	.74	.72
Boys	.63	.73	.70	.72
Girls	.67	.66	.71	.71

[a]$N = 6,651.$ [b]$N = 3,256.$

tion for the two states, for the four school grades, and by sex. The differences between Minnesota and Texas for the LM and LL scores show little consistent patterning. Similarly, no trend by grades is consistent over the four columns representing the two scores and the two states. Nor is there any consistent patterning by sex and by state. A comparison was made between these reliability coefficients for the first three years of the study, to see if there was any change as the study continued. A comparison was made between the fifth-grade values for the first, second, and third years of the study; these would include completely different sets of pupils. This check on trends that may have been operative, as the study continued indicated little in the way of consistent patterns of change. The same kind of study was made for sixth-grade pupils with the same results. A detailed table of these values, broken down by sex and by state, are given in Table 1 in Appendix B.

A Comparison of LM and LL Scores. The LM scores were based on four choices given each child, and the LL scores were based on two choices for each child. Hence, the LM scores would be expected to be somewhat more stable than the LL scores, and almost everywhere else in this study they correlated more highly with other variables than did the LL scores. It is thus a matter of some interest that the split-half reliabilities for LL scores are as high or higher than the LM scores. This was surprising in the light of experience with other correlations of these two scores. We do not know just why this happened.

ILLUSTRATIVE CASES

Experience has indicated that although a great deal can be communicated by general concepts, particular cases are needed to give a full picture of these children and their situations. These condensed descriptions of the behavior of individual children in the teachers' own words give a concrete and comprehensible picture of social interactions in complex and multivariate situations. In Minnesota, descriptions of boys and girls at different choice status levels were obtained through structured interviews with teachers. During the grade school period covered by this study, teachers normally had a single class of students for the entire day, so that they became better acquainted with the children than teachers ordinarily do in junior high and high schools. From each classroom, four interviews were obtained based on LM – LL scores (the lowest boy and girl, the highest boy or girl, and a middle child, opposite in sex to the high child). The interview outline is given on page 17.

One aim here is to show the differences in life situation between high- and low-choice children. Besides social adjustment, other important variables related to life situation are referred to — among them, sex of children, family factors, and socioeconomic status. Although age is an important developmental factor, our age range is, in general, too restricted to reveal major age differences in the kinds of behavior with which this project is concerned. However, school grade is given at the beginning of each case, following the child's name. SES was obtained by ranking each school according to the average income and education of the residents of each school district, using data from the 1960 census. This procedure treats SES as a continuous variable, and does not reveal sharp breaks or gaps between the subdivisions used. Sometimes differences in SES were related to marked differences in the children's behavior. On the other hand, some things, such as the personality characteristics of high-choice children, show little variation with socioeconomic level.

These interviews provide pictures of individual children as they appeared to their teachers, and are concrete examples of the children who will reappear as numbers in the statistical tables below.

Sometimes high-choice children seem to have an almost completely favorable combination of life situation and personality characteristics. They have, so to speak, all the assets, including adequate IQ. Their interpersonal behavior is commonly described as being friendly to everyone and easy to get along with; as sympathetic, considerate, kind, and helpful to others; as tolerant and showing good manners; and in line with some other studies of leadership, as being habitually fair in their dealings with others. With this pattern of characteristics, they seem to move through life with ease and with a minimum of friction. Joel and Lynn, both from the upper socioeconomic level, are children of this type.

><><><><

Joel (fifth grade) is a rather slight youngster, although he has good physical development. He is very neat and very clean.

This boy is unusually fair-minded. He is a very good, serious reader. He does not seem to have any special friends but seems to be well accepted by all.

On the playground he is well coordinated and interested in athletics. He has a real desire to be first and may have some difficulty accepting a third or fourth position on a team. He is very dependable at all times, very cooperative, and frequently chosen early.

In the classroom he is a very enthusiastic student, works well with others, and organizes things well whenever there is opportunity. Recently, when his group wrote a play, he helped organize the work.

His relationship to the teacher is also good. He generally takes suggestions quite well, although at times he may find it difficult. He seems to know his material quite well and is interested, but nevertheless may find it difficult to accept the fact that sometimes he also is wrong.

The youngsters seem to like him; they select him. Early in the year he was elected vice-president of the class. The children seem to react to him in a very positive way because he is a good student and yet not too domineering or aggressive. He seems to be very fair; he also has a great deal of enthusiasm.

The family places real emphasis on scholastic achievement. He has younger twin brothers and a brother in the fourth grade. The teacher does not know if there are other siblings. The father is in military service and apparently the children have been in this school for several years. It appears that the parents are quite exacting and perhaps put considerable pressure on Joel to achieve, but he seems to be adjusting to this pressure very well.

>>>>>>

Lynn (fourth grade) is a very beautiful child, well cared for, clean, and neat. She is very kind to all of the children, as well as to adults. She is of superior intelligence, is excellent in reading and writing, and is very creative.

On the playground Lynn enters in and is a leader. If there is any trouble, she tries to help before the teacher has to be called in. She uses excellent judgment. In the classroom she gets her work done and is very respectful to other people and their property. She treats everyone as if he is very important, which gains her many friends. To the teacher she is very respectful. Lynn is well accepted by the other children. It is felt that this is true because she is constantly aware of just being herself. She is very sharing and helpful.

She is from a very stable home that shows much interest in the school. The parents are interested in the child, cooperative with the school, and generally speaking, are quite adequate people.

>>>>>>

The correlation between the characteristics of the child and the characteristics of the family is positive, but by no means perfect. Frequently the high-choice children will come from an intact family situation which is described as close-knit, warm, and so forth, but this is not always the case. Ann and Ben are among these exceptions; they are also from an above average socioeconomic level.

Ann (fifth grade) is very well developed physically, mentally, emotionally, and educationally. She is very nice looking. She is well groomed, much more mature and conscious of her hair than most fifth-graders. She wears dainty feminine dresses.

Ann is very thoughtful of others. All children are fond of her except one or two less fortunate ones who may be a bit envious of what she has. She is very nice to other children, but does not "buy" friendships although she has much more money than most. The boys adore her, but she seems to pay little attention to them, at least to those in her own class. She definitely seems to be the leader of the class. When she gets an article of clothing, the others want the same thing. When she was in kindergarten, her teacher described her as "having a sense of responsibility, maturity of speech and actions, and a tendency to cooperate with others." The gym teacher reports that on the playground she is very well liked, average in skills, gets along well with others, is a potential leader, and at times has been assigned leadership jobs which she has carried through well.

She tries hard to do all of her assignments correctly. She is messy at home and her desk is never neat, but she always looks nice herself. She is always well behaved in the room and on the grounds.

Ann comes from a split home. Her parents are divorced, and the mother has remarried. However, there is still some friction with Ann's father. The mother is a very nice looking woman who works evenings as a hostess in one of the best restaurants. She gives Ann money and allows her to go shopping for her own clothes. She does a good job of selecting her own clothes, except for a tendency to make herself look a little older than she is. Since other girls her age are not permitted to do their own shopping, the other mothers do not permit their daughters to go shopping with Ann.

❧❧❧❧❧

Ben (fifth grade) is a short, but well-developed boy who is well cared for and clean. He is speedy and agile, with an elf-like face and a personality to match it. He is easy to get along with and agreeable to both his peers and his teacher. He is always interested in other people and has a real feeling for other children. Unpleasant situations embarrass or shame him. He is very gentle, kind, and considerate. He always allows things to upset him and he feels and acts sadly. At times he has converted these feelings into stomach pains.

On the playground he is all boy. He enjoys most activities and is enthusiastic. He is a little rough, but he wouldn't hurt anyone and the children realize this. He is especially fond of animals. He can be mischievous, but he is rarely mean. Occasionally he wastes time in the classroom, but when reprimanded is very ashamed. He is extremely understanding and perceptive of the classroom situation and of the children's feelings in relation to it.

With the teacher, he is cooperative, almost supportive. When he is reprimanded he feels bad, making the teacher feel guilty for having scolded him. He enjoys most subjects, but he has difficulty with arithmetic. Ben is a better than average student, and he has better than average ability. He works up to his capacity. In response to a composition assignment "Who Am I?" Ben wrote the following: "but most of all, I am a person who likes and helps all things." The teacher felt this was a fair evaluation.

Both boys and girls like him. They seek him out. They choose him readily for almost any activity. His sense of fairness and consideration for other children earn him widespread acceptance.

In earlier years, Ben's mother was highly regarded. She was a soft spoken, capable mother. Suddenly, the family split up and she divorced and remarried. This second marriage did not last and the mother was divorced again. She was remarried again within a year. During this period, the mother changed from a very mild person, on the surface at least, to a more aggressive, spitfire type. However, since Ben gets along so well in school, there has been no occasion for friction between the school and mother.

≈≈≈≈

Although there are differences in life conditions between socio-economic levels, and particularly between the top and bottom groups, there are many highly accepted children at all levels whose personality descriptions sound very similar. Ray and Marlene are high-choice children from the lowest socioeconomic group.

Ray (third grade) is a very neat, good-looking black boy. His body is just beautiful, so rythmic and balanced. He is mischievous at times, a real boy, but he is very easily handled by the teacher. He exemplifies good behavior and lightheartedness. His positive alertness is one main characteristic. He likes everyone and everything. In addition, he is interested in scientific things and does a lot of reading for further information. He is extremely fair, mature, and trustworthy. Ray's greatness is his healthy, wholesome mischievousness. He just plays more than anything else. He shows leadership qualities on the playground and in the classroom. Everyone seems to like him and he likes everyone else.

Ray respects authority and is a friend of the teacher. He has matured so that he is not saucy or disrespectful to teachers. He has an outgoing personality and uses good judgment in his relationships.

Ray is the oldest in the family. He assumes the responsibility of escorting his sister to school. He understands the family's budgeting situation and talks about it to the teacher. There are eight children in the family. His father is a construction man. His mother is at home all the time. She is very cooperative with the school. It seems to be a good, close-knit family.

≈≈≈≈≈

Marlene (fifth grade) is a large, tall, rather heavy girl who always comes to school very clean. She is a very mature, very active girl with a personality that seems older than her age. She can take on any responsibility and is admired very highly by the others, because she takes such good care of herself. She is a good leader, and gets along extra well with adults. She is a very outgoing child but sometimes is sensitive when she feels that she is not living up to her standards.

She mixes well on the playground, loves sports, and takes them seriously, but her mother says that at home she doesn't play outside often. Her physical coordination is fair. Because of her large size, she is not good in tumbling, and that type of activity.

She achieves very well, and likes to achieve. Others recognize her as being superior and seek her out. She is very popular and is almost always chosen first in everything, with the possible exception of dancing. With her teacher, she always speaks very kindly and is always very mannerly. She can handle almost any situation. The children in the class who want to do well always want her in their group. She is nice to everybody, does not tattle, but is also not the type who likes to go in clans.

Marlene has many home responsibilities. Her mother is divorced. She works as a waitress and at times has held down two jobs. The mother, too, seems to be a very independent type of person. There are five children in the family, and Marlene is number three.

≈≈≈≈≈

Some children are able to gain high acceptance from their peers in spite of one or two characteristics which would seem to be handicaps. These children have enough positive attributes to overcome the effects of such liabilities. The following descriptions emphasize that the high-choice children are not all completely problem-free.

Alex (third grade) is a tall youngster who is mature and superior in all aspects. He is actually on a fifth-grade level in social behavior, physical maturity, and classwork. He is very intelligent, and very sensitive and understanding with other people. His one weakness is stuttering, which does interfere with his achievement.

On the playground and in the gym, Alex is well coordinated and superior in ability. In the classroom there are no problems. He has good work habits and is very friendly to all the other youngsters. He is humble and doesn't try to assert himself or make known his superior ability. He is respectful to the teacher. He is anxious to learn and curious about many things.

There is some change in Alex's behavior this year as he is becoming more aware of his stuttering. He gets disgusted with it now. He is a bright, capable youngster who has good ability provided he gets some help for his stuttering before it comes to be destructive to his self-confidence. The speech correctionist says that at this point it would not help to work on the stuttering problem.

The other children respect him very much. They ask him for help, and they admire his ability as well as the sympathetic understanding and thoughtfulness he expresses for them.

Alex is an only child and his parents are divorced. His mother is a very independent person. She works, reads widely, travels a great deal, and the two of them go on many excursions together. She is a Cub Scout den mother. Alex and his mother live with the grandmother, who is a typist. Alex seems to have no contact with his father; he has never talked about him, and the mother has never mentioned him at all.

⋙⋘

Gloria (third grade) is a nice looking blonde girl of average height. She is always neat and clean with her hair fixed. She is a quiet girl but has a good sense of humor. She smiles a lot. On the other hand, if she is criticized, she pouts, is stubborn, and won't do anything. She is somewhat underhanded and seems like a double person. She seems to cooperate very well, but the minute you turn your back she is doing just the opposite. Once her mother came to school and explained what a problem Gloria was. Before this the teacher had not noticed that the girl did things when her back was turned, but after the mother's visit, the teacher started to pay attention and realized that the mother perhaps had been correct. She has a very innocent look on her face when she does something she shouldn't. The mother says she beats up her sisters and tells lies at home. The mother is at the point where she doesn't believe anything Gloria says.

In gym class she is well coordinated, she is chosen for teams, and she plays pretty fairly. She pouts if she loses, but she does not give up very easily.

She is a good worker in the classroom. She tends to talk to kids next to her more than the other children do. She is just barely hanging on in the top reading group; she is slipping down toward the middle. Even if she doesn't have too much to say, she always volunteers to recite. She obeys the teacher but most of the time very reluctantly. If she is talking to a neighbor and the teacher asks her to turn around, she turns around very, very slowly and it takes a great deal of patience to wait for her to do this.

She plays with the boys mostly. The girls liked her up until about a month ago when they were giving a play; she apparently couldn't have her way and they asked her to leave. This is the first time that they have outwardly rejected her. They have been rather friendly to her. She seems as though she is very shy, but actually underneath all this she is quite aggressive. She is soft spoken but she often initiates the conversation.

There is a stepfather in the home. Gloria is the only child by her first father. They wanted to take her to a child guidance clinic for examination, but the father refused and the stepfather is not at all cooperative.

≈≈≈≈≈

The low-choice or least-liked children show various patterns of behavior which attract negative choices. Perhaps the most common of these is a set of characteristics more or less opposite to those of the high-choice children. Instead of being generally friendly and considerate, they are pests, complaining, quarrelsome, critical, touchy, domineering, poor sports, and sometimes inclined to force themselves on others. Examples of behavior in this area by boys and girls at various socioeconomic levels are as follows.

Leroy (fifth grade) is very tall and heavyset, an attractive boy with good posture. He torments other boys sadistically by teasing and hitting them, mostly picking on others who are in a lower grade. He could be a better than average student scholastically if he would apply himself, but he is in the lowest reading group. He tends to break up or socially disintegrate when he is in any higher reading group.

On the playground, he participates well in games and seems to like to get involved. He has average athletic skill. In the classroom he tends to torment other children by hitting or punching them.

Leroy does fairly good schoolwork in the classroom. He can be pleasant to others, but he generally is somewhat reserved in his social relationships. Other than his teasing and punching, Leroy seems to be unresponsive to most of the others in the room. He has built a small shell around himself. He gets along well with the teacher, and he seems to like her attention. His behavior has been getting better in that he seems to feel more comfortable in the school situation. The more able students in the class tend to ignore him, while the less able tend to report him for behavioral infractions and to dislike him. He feels inferior and this is sensed by the group. He is always a follower, even though he shows some signs of high ability.

His mother is very concerned about him. The mother is a very intelligent person who seems to understand Leroy's social plight. The school has had no contact with the father.

&&&&&&

Jacob (fifth grade) is an awkward boy with poor posture. He is large in the hips and slouches and never sits up straight. He is unkempt and his clothes are dirty. He seems weird. He is quite intelligent, has original ideas, and does good work if it does not involve tedious tasks or drill. He has many fears, such as fear of the dark. He tries to be comical and is regarded as the clown of his family. He has his own science collection and hobbies. He has traveled a lot and has more general information than most children.

On the playground he does not participate in sports. He is chosen last for team games. He has one friend at a time, and the two of them will run around the playground provoking fights. The friend will be very close with him and the friendship will continue for a long time. Other children either do not notice him or call him a dope. The girls sometimes call him names and he will hit them in the back. He pays them back ten times what they did to him. He has trouble with police boys and other people in authority. Recently he was beaten up by the police boys. Once he rode his bike to school to avoid the police boys and was deliberately hit in a head-on collision by another boy on a bike.

He likes to make jokes about teachers. Despite his smarting off he has a good relationship with the teacher. He likes to just talk about science with her. He is volunteering more often in class. The children respect him for the information he has and they sometimes choose him for committee work. They do not understand his kind of humor. He is a renegade and revolutionist.

33

His father is a high school teacher. The parents are very intellectual people but are not practical. Humdrum household tasks are neglected while the parents are reading books. The mother brought a psychology book to the school conference. The father has droopy posture similar to Jacob's. He is interesting and friendly, but there is some gossip that family relationships are not smooth.

≈≈≈≈≈

When Calvin (third grade) was mentioned his teacher smiled. He is the biggest boy by far in the room, and is sloppy, dirty, and wears poor clothing. He makes his appearance even worse by rubbing chalk all over his face and by making pencil marks on his hands and neck. The children do not like him. When asked why, the teacher laughed and said that she doesn't like him either. He is obnoxious, angers easily, has a big chip on his shoulder, loves to fight, and picks fights both on the playground and in the building.

The others do not like to play with him, partly because of his poor coordination, but mostly because he is a poor sport, argues, and has a big mouth. He knows and uses many dirty words, so girls, especially, do not like him. He really has no friends. On the playground he is chosen last or sits and watches the others play.

In the classroom he doesn't do his work. He walks around sneering when told to sit down, or just sits with a smirk on his face. He has above average ability and could do classwork. He has been sent to the principal because of misbehavior and not working. He shows interest only in discussions and may contribute to these, showing that he does have quite a background of knowledge in science and current events. He likes music and sings very well.

The teacher felt that he may have changed some for the better this year. However, he has not accepted her help to try to work through some of his personality problems. She has not met his parents, but has been told that both are alcoholics. They own a lake cabin, and Calvin tells of boating and fishing with his father. His siblings are older, and all are married. Calvin is the tag end, the unwanted child, the last one at home. He seems to be a very unhappy, angry boy.

[NOTE: Calvin participated in all four years of the study. He received *no* LM choices during the third, fourth, fifth, and sixth grades.]

≈≈≈≈≈

Suzy (third grade) has a very pretty face but is quite obese, sad looking, and very untidy. She is most characterized by her desire to be noticed or loved. However, she constantly pushes others aside, always wants to be first, and does not know how to get along with other youngsters.

On the playground, Suzy feels rejected. She cannot play as well as the others. She constantly makes excuses for this. She feels quite left out. She wants to win all the time but is a very poor loser.

The classroom situation is much the same. She is of average intelligence and has made good progress in her work, but she is extremely disruptive, and the classroom is only one of many places where she goes and disrupts. She pushes other children out of the way to make room for herself. She is a thorn in the side of the other youngsters, chiefly because of her constant bids for attention.

In the eyes of adults, she is a very pathetic youngster who cannot seem to conquer some of her feelings. She relates very badly to other people. At first, Suzy lipped off to the teacher, made constant bids for attention, and felt she was treated differently from the others. She has a long way to go before she will get as much acceptance as any child needs. There are times when Suzy can be quite sweet, but most of the time she is just a noise box, full of belligerence and hostility.

Suzy is a social as well as a psychological mess. She is extremely rejected by her peer group. It is doubtful whether she has even one close friend. She tries so hard to gain attention and acceptance but just does not know how. Her family and home life have definitely contributed to this.

Suzy's parents, especially her mother, have tried to cooperate with the school. They have helped her with reading and she has shown some improvement, but she is a very rejected child. In fact, all of her siblings are rejected. Neither mother nor father are interested in children, but they had them so they are stuck with them. Suzy has a lot of responsibility for a younger sister who is severely handicapped. It is far too much responsibility for a child, and she feels hostile about this.

❧❧❧❧❧

Carla (fourth grade) is a small, messy child who is not clean or neat. She has the face of a little old lady. Her impish appearance is different from the other children. This child has low mental ability; her IQ is about 85.

On the playground she teases other youngsters and pokes them to get their attention and to get them to chase her. She is not a good team member and seems to have little interest in games.

In the classroom Carla is well behaved and works, but in a

rather messy way. She makes little contribution to the classwork. She provokes attention by nudging her classmates or by playfully taking their pencils. Carla's relationship with the teacher is fairly good. The children are irritated with Carla and they generally dislike her. They never pick her as a partner either for group work or team activities.

The family has financial difficulties. There are seven or eight children. Her older brothers have also been school problems.

❦❦❦❦❦

A second group of characteristics of the least-liked children has to do with poor conduct; to act disruptively in the classroom, to be defiant of the teacher, or to participate in offenses such as stealing. Other items under this heading are: unreliable, cheats, difficult to control, disruptive, shouts out in class, and is a classroom problem. This overlaps the first set of objectionable interpersonal behaviors listed above. It has more emphasis on rebelling against authority and less on antagonizing other children.

Sammy (fifth grade) is a small, very messy boy. His skin and clothes are always dirty. He writes nasty notes and the girls complain about his behavior. He often sits in class and kisses magazine pictures. He has a very filthy mind. He brings many playthings to school, as well as candy and food. His work habits are very poor. He often talks out of turn. He is one of the first to boo in an auditorium.

In gym he is well coordinated but a very poor sport. He gets into fights easily and bends the rules to suit his own needs.

In the classroom he talks out of turn in a deep, loud voice. He is a great attention seeker. He is disturbing to others and cannot stay in his seat. He could be an average student, but he is in the low average group. He doesn't seem to be able to get anything done in class. He cannot follow directions.

He is disliked by the girls particularly, because of his language. Some of the boys do not like him because of his impulsive behavior and because he talks too much. He has two friends, but even they don't mind if he is not there.

The teacher cannot get through to him. She can scold, she can isolate him, she can do anything — nothing seems to have any effect.

Sammy's family background is very poor. His brother was sent to the county training school for stealing. There are two uneducatable children in the home with IQ's around 45. Sammy's IQ is about 79. The family has been involved with the police many times. Once the mother and her sons were picked up in their car by the police because they had stolen a whole back seat full of groceries. They had to threaten to impound the car before she let them open it. The family is the type that have the neighbors call them to wake them up rather than buying an alarm clock. It is a very difficult family to work with because they have borderline mentality.

❧❧❧❧❧

Shirley (fifth grade) is a very large, overweight, slow-moving, lethargic youngster. She's very messy and generally not too clean. She has many personality problems. She is very bossy, demands her own way, and refuses to give in if she doesn't get it. Someone is always picking on her, she says, with no recognition of her own involvement in any difficulties. She has a real need for attention, going almost daily to the nurse with one ailment or another. Shirley has been picking up things in the classroom that do not belong to her. She can lie with a perfectly straight face, even when she's holding the stolen object in her hand. There have been a great many police line difficulties, so she goes home by herself now.

In the classroom she's talking constantly. She has a very limited attention span, always demanding attention from the teacher by raising her hand, talking out loud, pushing other youngsters, going up to sharpen her pencils, and so forth. The youngsters really dislike Shirley, and the teacher admits he, too, finds it difficult to like her. She does so many bothersome things that it is sometimes difficult to find a positive feature to work on. She is, however, respectful to him and never talks back. She sometimes carries out directions, but generally it's been a very difficult, trying year for all involved. Academically, Shirley could do much better than she is doing. She is in the lower third of the class. She finds it difficult to complete assignments. Instead of asking questions when she does not understand, she will merely sit.

The family situation is very disorganized. The father has been out of the home for some time; there are numerous children and several of the older ones have been delinquent. Currently, two of her brothers are on probation. Shirley says she was raised in beer joints and given little attention by her parents. This apparently continues to be true. The mother has had no contact with the school, has not been responsive to suggestions, and generally has appeared rather disinterested in Shirley. The family has been receiving casework help for many years from various social agencies.

37

≈≈≈≈≈

Occasionally, the previously described negative inter-individual behavior is accompanied by withdrawal. These children, when they do relate to other children, seem to do everything wrong — they can be pests, sarcastic, touchy, in much the same way as the aggressive children. However, their negative behavior is often accompanied by a lethargic, detached, indifferent, or withdrawn manner. Occasionally, although they might annoy other children in the classroom, they seem not to want to join in playground activities. Or, they might be withdrawn in the classroom but aggressive on the playground.

Fred (fourth grade) is a small, slight, pale boy who walks and runs with a slight limp because of a leg that was broken a few years ago. He is a very quiet, withdrawn boy who participates very little in class. His mother said that when he was in another school, the teachers laughed at his awkwardness, which made him very withdrawn and unwilling to participate in group discussion. He gets angry very easily. Most of his anger is directed toward other children and only occasionally at the teacher.

At times, Fred can be very pleasant and he sometimes has very good ideas in class. He asks some interesting questions, particularly in science, which interests him very much. However, he is not a particularly good student and has repeated a grade.

Fred is not very well liked by other children, and is usually one of the last chosen for games. He is not a very good sport, and he becomes quite angry if made to leave the game because of an error. He associates with two or three boys who are also rather slow in class, but at any one time he seems unable to relate to more than one child. His usual behavior consists of hitting out at others either verbally or physically. However, Fred on occasion shows an unusual sensitivity to others' feelings. For instance, one day when he threw a ball and hit a girl in the nose, and she began to cry, he went over to her without any prompting to say that he was sorry and hoped that she was not hurt.

In class, he often creates a disturbance in spite of the fact that most of the children get after him about his behavior. He is well controlled when doing something that really interests him, but it is extremely difficult to get him interested in everyday lessons. He will just say "I don't want to do it." He is, however, trying to participate more in class discussions. During the lunch period, however, he constantly runs around the building getting into mischief.

Fred would like to have friends and seems to try, but he does not have the know-how to develop real, meaningful friendships. Instead he is aggressive, verbally abusive, and sarcastic. The children react negatively to him.

Fred's family moved here this year. His parents are separated. His mother works during the night and sleeps most of the day, so there is not much chance for Fred to develop a close relationship with her. She seems overprotective of him in a rather negative way, and defends him regardless of what he may have done, without any real understanding or positive guidance.

✖✖✖✖✖

Elizabeth (third grade) is very shoddy, dirty, and drools at times. She daydreams a good deal and rarely fits into the group activity of the class. She has poor speech habits and talks baby talk. She may pout and stamp her feet as well. She has average ability, craves attention, and wants to please, but her achievement is very poor. She likes to help the teacher, but she does a poor job.

On the playground her behavior is fairly good. She plays a position like goalie and tries hard.

In the room she wanders and daydreams. She behaves at a much more immature level than the other children. If she could be rocked and cuddled, she would be happy. In reading she is working in a simple alphabet book. She used to throw tantrums but is leaving misbehavior in favor of just sitting and not doing much work. She is improving slowly, but she is so dirty, and everything that she does is so messy that the children do not want to touch anything that she handles. She pokes them, asks silly questions, and interrupts them. They reject her and are generally unhappy with her. She seems to like everybody, however.

She tries hard at home, and can take some responsibility. Because of her mother's illness, Elizabeth spent a year on a farm with an aunt and uncle. She is back home now, but she is living the life on the farm in her thinking. Her mother frequently writes notes to the teacher about Elizabeth, but rarely follows up on any suggestions. Elizabeth seems to be happy considering all the responsibilities that she has at home.

✖✖✖✖✖

Many poorly accepted children are characterized by extreme passivity or a tendency to withdraw from contacts with other children. Some seem to use their withdrawal in an almost active manner as a means of shutting others out of their lives.

Andy (sixth grade) is very unattractive. He is large and untidy, with extremely poor posture, poor facial features, and poor muscular coordination. When you look at him, you immediately know that something is wrong. There is a slight disfigurement about his face.

His intelligence is average, but he is very withdrawn and will not initiate any conversation. He will give only a minimum answer to a question. He is passive; his classmates consider him cold. He is a pathetic youngster.

Despite his poor coordination, he is good at baseball and he gets most of his acceptance there. He has little or no enthusiasm however. He just plays along with no emotion and no animation in what he is doing. It seems he could not care less.

He is never with the others in their classwork. He does not listen and consequently gets things wrong. He and the teacher have a very good relationship although Andy is still not very communicative.

He is very passive and nonaggressive toward all the children, but is very negative with them. He does not care much about them, apparently, or feel that he can talk very well with them. They accept him as being there and that is about it. They do not want much to do with him because there is not much there to be with. They feel that they can certainly get along without him.

Andy has a smaller twin brother, who is duller than he, but a little more outgoing. He comes from a matriarchal family. The mother is the boss. She is quite outspoken and is always ready to tell the teachers off. She says that the father belittles the boy. She thinks that her kids can do no wrong. The father is very quiet, but probably has to be. He has little or no vitality and is quite unexpressive.

≈≈≈≈≈

Margaret (fourth grade) is a very beautiful child but very shy and quiet. She shows no personality but is poker-faced and deadpan. She does not smile at others and shows no curiosity in the classroom. Her intelligence is average, but she daydreams in class and does not always know her assignments. She does not laugh at jokes. She locks herself within herself. The mother said that Margaret is loud and active at home, but this seems doubtful because she is just as poker-faced with her Girl Scout troop. She shows no response either on the playground or in the room. The children do not choose her. She volunteers no ideas. She is like a board. The teacher could not make her smile or get mad no matter what she said to her in the whole year. She does recite, but she does so in a stilted fashion.

Margaret comes from a large family crowded into a small house. The parents are not educated people. All the members of the family seem a little odd. An older sister is also withdrawn, but seems nastier than Margaret. Her mother is a nice looking woman who had a sugar-sweet attitude toward the teacher when she came for a conference. It is said that the father makes severe criticisms of the school.

⚡⚡⚡⚡⚡

Dean (sixth grade) is a neat, well dressed, pleasant, quite handsome boy of average size. He habitually fails to complete assignments. He is a dreamer, but when he does any work it is quite well done. He seems to have considerable ability in math and language, but his main interest is in music.

In the building and in the classroom he is very quiet and unconcerned. In fact, it is quite difficult to describe him since he seems so much of a nonentity. He is not particularly troublesome, although he may occasionally whisper.

The children tend to ignore Dean; they neither like him nor dislike him. He can be quite nice to the teacher. He sometimes has a blank look in class, flounders and seems to be lost, and does not get his work done.

Dean's only close friend is also rejected by the other children. The youngsters do not accept Dean because he seems lusterless, unconcerned, and is somewhat of a dreamer.

The parents are concerned; the mother has been active in the PTA. He has a younger brother who does better work in school.

⚡⚡⚡⚡⚡

The preceding examples of negative, withdrawn children are different from those showing simple shyness. Many children relate positively to others but are not very outgoing. These children might be described as shy, timid, quiet, aloof, unassertive, or as willing to join in games but not likely to initiate them. They are typical of a large group of children who often are found in the middle in terms of peer acceptance-rejection. Henry, Kathy, and Larry are examples of middle children. They can, occasionally, appear as high-choice children, as does Craig, whose interview is also included here.

Henry (fourth grade) is neat, clean, but not well dressed. The most important thing about him is that he is very shy. He is a good citizen, willing, cooperative, and will probably never have any extreme behavior problems, but will find life somewhat difficult because of inability to assert himself. He follows directions of others on the playground and doesn't have any obnoxious behavior. He has average coordination and is able to participate. In the classroom he is very passive. He gets his work done, has average ability, and occasionally will volunteer. His relationship to the teacher is good, there seem to be no antiauthority feelings. He follows directions well and has never caused any problem in the classroom.

As far as his reaction to other youngsters, Henry has friends, including one close one, but he finds it very difficult to reach out and be friendly to other people. Other children accept him but don't seek him out because of his passive, placid approach to life. People tend to forget about him because he's so quiet and unassertive.

There are six children in the family and Henry is in the middle. The mother seems very interested at conferences, but has not revealed any family problems and no particular family strengths.

❧❧❧❧❧

Kathy (fifth grade) is a shy, soft-spoken girl of average intelligence. She is a very poor student. In a recent achievement test she was about average on national norms, whereas most of the class were up around the ninetieth percentile. She lacks confidence, is afraid that she might say the wrong thing, and seems to fear the sound of her own voice. While she seems able to read all right, she has poor comprehension. Her parents do not seem to understand the need for good comprehension and argue that if she is a good reader that is that. She has a great deal of trouble with arithmetic and blocks at times, making improvements only to lose them.

Kathy plays well with the other children and reacts well to them, but she is introverted and lacking in skills and confidence. She seems to be afraid to seek out the teacher. Her classmates make fun of her occasionally, and laugh when she makes some incorrect answer. This seems to be very upsetting to her. She is not unpopular, however, and some members of the class seek her out. She is definitely not the last one chosen in games.

Kathy is the youngest child in her family, with two much older brothers. The parents tend to baby her, and in a sense contribute to her diffidence. When things are not going well in school, she often pleads sickness, and the parents have allowed her to stay home until the teacher made an issue and required that she come back to school. Both parents come in for parent interviews.

✎✎✎✎

Larry (sixth grade) is an attractive boy who is always well dressed and clean and gives the impression of being well cared for. He is very quiet and retiring, not at all aggressive. He never calls attention to himself when the children are choosing sides. He never waves his hands and says "pick me" the way the other children do. He is so soft spoken the teacher often has to ask him to repeat things. He lacks confidence and seems to be aware that he is not doing as well as other children. His IQ is not high and he is a very slow learner. His eyes usually have a sort of blank expression, as if he does not understand.

On the playground he does well in sports, especially softball, and the boys seem to like him. He's kindly, sweet, and smiles in an attractive friendly way. He's not at the end of the list when sides are chosen, and the other children always say that they like him.

In the classroom he conforms well. It might be better if he'd be a little mischievous just to show a little life. In relation to the other students, Larry is very retiring and not quite able to ask for a place for himself. He always uses a minimum of words, and it is necessary for both children and adults to draw things out of him. He is always very courteous and mannerly to the teacher. The teacher said she almost wishes there were something she could scold him for, just as a sign of a normal child. He seems very anxious to please the teacher, perhaps to compensate for his lack of academic skill. Now he is seated next to a boy who is very bright and who seems to be drawing him out a bit. This association probably won't last in junior high because of the differences in ability between the two boys. The typical reaction of the other students toward Larry is that they like him, but are not always aware of him because of his quiet manner. He has never done anything to make others dislike him. He is always very courteous, but is extremely retiring.

Larry's mother realizes that he is slow, but says that she has the same problem so is unable to help with his schoolwork. The teacher said that the mother did not come to conferences, and had come to only one open house. She looked at some of Larry's work and commented that it was hard for her too.

✎✎✎✎

Craig (third grade) is a nice-looking, average-sized boy. He is very smart, extremely talented in art, and creative in anything he does. You would notice him in the classroom because he is so busy with his work that he pays no attention to anyone else. He is almost on the shy side. He is very shy with the teacher, rarely starts a conversation, and when he has to get up in front of the room, he looks embarrassed and very much as though he wished he were not in the limelight.

In sports, he is average, but he has such a marvelous disposition. He never loses his temper and has the most fantastic, subtle sense of humor for his age that keeps the teacher laughing and which both adults and children appreciate.

He is very popular with the children. He never becomes angry no matter what they do. In fact, this almost becomes a fault. He lets lots of things go until he is really provoked; then instead of speaking up or fighting back, he tends to walk away so other children sometimes take advantage of him. However, he is always among the first chosen even though he is not the best player. He is such a good loser and jokes constantly.

His behavior in the classroom is good. He rarely has to be told not to do anything or to get to work. When he is given a job or an assignment to do, he concentrates.

There has been no change this year. He was definitely popular with both boys and girls last year, and this year he is much the best-liked child in the room.

He has a brother in fifth grade who is extremely bright and very competitive with Craig. There is also a younger boy in kindergarten. It is a normal family situation. The father is a builder, the mother a housewife. They are above average in financial circumstances and have a lake cottage, a cabin cruiser, and a swimming pool. They have taken trips all over the United States. The parents are very interested in school and in their boys' grades. Because the boys have had much experience with travel, books, and magazines, they contribute more in the classroom than most children.

⋙⋘

Many of the middle children are seen as having a mixture of positive and negative characteristics. They have neither enough assets to gain high acceptance for themselves nor severe enough liabilities to cause them to be rejected. In a majority of cases, children in this middle group received relatively few choices, positive or negative. It was rare for a child to receive a relatively large number of *both* positive and negative choices (e.g., seven positive and four negative).

Tony (fifth grade) is clean and quite handsome. He is a very pleasing and pleasant child who tends to be an extrovert. He is well coordinated and athletic. He is curious about many things, and if he is motivated toward learning, he is full of life and energy and vitality. He does not usually work to capacity, however. His intelligence is about average. Tony likes attention at all times and wants to be the center of things. He tries to be a leader in any direction and he is often an aggressive self-appointed leader, especially in playground games. He has a short attention span. He interrupts whenever he feels like it. He disregards rules of being quiet in lines, in the halls, and so on. He is clever but immature and often acts silly. He is a poor sport if he does not get his way. He accepts rebuke poorly. Sometimes he will stalk off in anger. He tends to be a bit rough on the playground, but he is a good player.

Actually, Tony gets along quite well with the other children. He has a good sense of humor and is quite enthusiastic. He seems to take kidding well and often gives it out. He is very daring and will try almost anything. He is willing to take suggestions from the teacher, and responds to discipline sometimes, but he soon falls back to his previous ways. He sees the teacher as an authority figure and that is about all.

His carelessness seems to get him in more and more minor trouble with things that might have been more acceptable when he was younger. Generally, however, he is liked by the other students. He is aggressive, daring, imaginative, and all boy. He is often chosen first for games.

The parents have been separated from time to time. This is a kind of an on-again, off-again proposition. The father is irresponsible; he works occasionally and has been described by others as a kind of happy-go-lucky fellow. The parents have trouble handling Tony. The mother has difficulty in setting limits for him. Tony is a middle child and is without close companions at home.

❧❧❧❧❧❧

Cynthia (sixth grade) wears gobs of makeup, tries to do very difficult hairdos, and looks rather wild and terrible at times. She wears extremely short skirts. She is a little heavy and a little on the short side compared with the other girls. She is a good student and a good worker, but if she doesn't like something she will withdraw from it.

Her relationships and behavior on the playground are good, although she cannot run fast, and the boys tease her about this. Cynthia laughs about the teasing rather than getting upset about it.

45

Her behavior in the classroom is fine, and no problems were noted in this area. Cynthia does not go out of her way to do things for her classmates; her closest friends are outside of school and older than she is. She has no problems with the teacher.

Boys tend to tease her, sometimes about her extreme hairdos. The other girls' reactions to Cynthia are rather neutral; they do not go out of their way to be with her nor do they go out of their way to get away from her. They more or less passively accept her and there are no signs of outward rejection.

The school knows nothing about the family.

⋙⋘

Tom (third grade) is a nice-looking, average-sized, healthy boy. He is on top intellectually, expresses himself very well, and can do extremely good work. He has an unusually good vocabulary, is interested in many subjects, and has a sense of humor. He often volunteers to explain things and do things in class, yet he seems to be something of an introvert. He is not entirely sure of himself in group activities, though he is confident doing things by himself.

In games his coordination is good, he likes to play, and is chosen, but he is definitely not a leader and until recently has been a very poor loser. He has a fear of doing things wrong, and is hesitant, slow, and deliberate in his responses until he's absolutely certain they're right. In the past he has been a tattletale, and as a result has been very much disliked. This seems definitely related to his sensitivity and insecurity. This year he has an improved attitude toward others and is gradually getting to be more liked. He has no definite enemies, but the kids are somewhat indifferent toward him most of the time. This seems to be largely because he is not fully outgoing.

The father, a professor, seems to be overambitious for him. There is evidence that both parents pressure him to do things. Tom is the youngest child, and his father is relatively old for a parent. Evidently there is quite a rigid schedule for him at home. However, the parents do spend a lot of time with Tom, talking things over and filling him in with information.

⋙⋘

Teresa (fifth grade) is a very tall, very overweight girl. She's not very well coordinated in her walk. She has poor eyesight and needs glasses but rarely wears them. She has a pretty face but her eyes seem small because of her weight. Her enthusiasm and generally good sense of humor distinguish her. Her size does not seem to affect her. Academically she's above average. She discourages rather quickly, but responds eagerly to help and encouragement. She has a happy-go-lucky disposition and attitude toward life.

On the playground Teresa is considered a good group member. She is often the brunt of jokes because of her poor coordination, but this does not seem to bother her. She is fair and demands fairness from other children.

In the classroom she gets along very well. Her enthusiasm carries through in discussions and she contributes a great deal of information. Because she is brighter than many of the other children, she likes to do a lot of independent work and takes a great deal of pride in her accomplishments. She is thoughtful of others and has a good, pleasing personality. She's well liked by the children, primarily because of her good sense of humor. She is not a leader, but not a complete follower either. She responds to positive leadership and creates a little of it herself.

Teresa is eager to conform to class discipline, and responds to any friendly approaches that the teacher might make. She can handle responsibility well and as a result is given quite a bit. She follows directions intelligently. She minds her own business and does what is expected of her.

Teresa's mother is active in PTA and assumes a great deal of responsibility in the community.

≈≈≈≈≈

Another group of disliked or rejected children includes those whose behavior toward other children is not extremely negative, aggressive, or withdrawn, but who have other liabilities which seem impossible for them to overcome, even though they may have relatively inoffensive personalities. These unfavorable factors include low IQ, poor physical coordination, poor appearance, messy or sloppy dress, body odor, physical disabilities, and unfavorable family situations.

Evelyn (third grade) is a very cute average-sized youngster with long corkscrew curls. She's neat and well kept and relatively prissy about herself. Her appearance is sometimes irritating because she is always so perfectly dressed and tends to feel that she is a little better than the rest. She is a dull child and a very poor reader. She does not stand out in the group at all. She is very polite and willing, however. She's good in arithmetic but cannot transfer from the book to other situations.

On the playground she plays fair, but is not too enthusiastic. In the classroom she's quiet and unresponsive. She gets her work done, but it is 90 per cent wrong because she can't read. She cheats unless the teacher watches her. She minds the teacher but does not respond or communicate.

She usually latches onto one classmate and has a more or less "I don't care" attitude toward the rest. She does not get along well in the group. Evelyn is accepted by the other students to a point; however, she's not chosen often and not noticed a good deal. It is felt this is because she is basically shy, and does not have too much to offer them because of her low intelligence. She is a sitter, not jovial, but rather an apathetic child.

The mother came to one parent-teacher conference late in the year. She has to work. She too is noncommunicative. She is relatively defensive about Evelyn, and at the same time she is rather unconcerned and does not appear to have a good deal of interest in her school adjustment.

❧❧❧❧❧

Bernie (sixth grade) and school are just not compatible. He is a rather untidy boy, has dirty clothes, and is frequently a mess. His eyes are very expressive, he seems to have a nice personality and an easy way, and he cooperates as much as he knows how. However, he is slow in reading, and has very poor study habits. His IQ is about 85.

Bernie's coordination is very good, and he is very much at home on the playground. His greatest achievement lies here, and he gets along well with the others.

In class he seems to be getting more negative, doesn't apply himself, and gives up easily. Still, there is no particular misbehavior except occasional talking. He is very much interested in the rest of the class, wants to be friendly with them and wants very much to keep up with them. His special friends are other members of the slow group. He is easily hurt by others and very easily led. He talks with the teacher quite a bit, expresses a desire to do anything she asks, and is very apologetic if he has not done quite the right thing. He will try to do things, but fails, and there has been more misbehavior recently.

Other children seem to reject him because he does poorly; they never choose him in the classroom. Often he does the wrong thing just to get attention. They seem to realize what he is trying to do, and openly dislike it.

The family is very poor and on welfare. There are quite a few children. The father drinks. The mother tries to cooperate. She uses a sister in the same classroom as an informant about what Bernie is doing. The sister is very bright and Bernie shows a great deal of resentment toward her.

⨯⨯⨯⨯⨯⨯

Arthur (third grade) is considerably overweight and not very attractive. He does not have a very happy look on his face, and his expression shows little warmth or feeling. His total manner, attitude, and appearance have many negative qualities. He has lost some weight, is always neat and very well dressed, but he has very poor coordination; he walks very slowly like a big fat man and is very clumsy. Arthur is quite different from the other children. There is something about him which is negative. He is, in a sense, messy, yet his clothes are clean. Nothing seems to fit just right on him. Everything he does is messy and unclean. Any books that he has had for a short time look worn and dirty.

He has about average ability. He reads quite well and is in the average reading group. He seems to want to please the teacher and do a good job. There is something likable about Arthur to adults.

On the playground Arthur participates fairly well and is able to compete somewhat. He's not the last to be chosen. His coordination has improved as he has lost weight. He seems to be less aggressive toward other youngsters than he was previously. He has, however, been called to task for using filthy language at times. His dirty language to older girls has been somewhat startling. There is something about his manner that is uncouth and almost repulsive at times. The other youngsters do not seem particularly interested in Arthur. They tolerate him at best.

The family has considerable difficulty in adjusting to the community. This is a high income community and the family simply does not fit in. They have had many financial problems, partly due to poor budgeting. The father has been working with the paternal grandfather and his salary is very low. The parents, about two years ago, were particularly dependent upon a social agency; the mother called the social worker at all hours of the day. The father is a rather ill-mannered, uncouth person who is not very bright. Arthur's younger sister in the second grade is of special class [retarded] ability. The parents have been regressive in some ways and seem to try to buy friendship and favors from the teacher. The children constantly bring candy bars, cupcakes, and so on to school to treat the others.

⨯⨯⨯⨯⨯⨯

LaDonna (fifth grade) is a tall, attractive girl who is at least one year older than the others. She is very sloppy and unclean, but she has a winning smile and a quick sense of humor, and is a very likable girl. Her attendance is extremely irregular and her school achievement is poor. She is physically and emotionally much more mature than the other youngsters. She has received very little socialization from home, and operates on the principle of having a good time.

On the playground, LaDonna is a very good sport. She plays fair and tries to help kids. She is not rowdy, especially when supervised, and she knows how to share.

In the classroom she is not attentive, and needs constant motivation. She is quite irresponsible. She has an artistic flair which sometimes gains her popularity, but she has an "I don't care" attitude at an early age.

LaDonna always has friends and is helpful and warm to youngsters; however, they know that she is really not the kind of girl they should play with. Many parents have told their children absolutely to stay away from LaDonna because she is known to steal and lead kids into difficulty.

LaDonna has very little respect for authority, is sassy, and is out to get but not to give. She seems to have learned not to steal in school. She will eventually appear in juvenile court. She has little motivation to change, is unconcerned about her behavior, and will definitely go on through life with problems.

LaDonna is the charmer type and is accepted to some degree by the others. She is rejected by the nicer kids because they know they shouldn't like such a girl, but this doesn't have any effect on her. She has a few friends who supply her with a good time, and she knows how to manufacture a good time for herself.

The mother and father live in separate cities, but are supposedly still married. They're very nomadic people. For the past several years LaDonna's mother has moved back and forth between cities, and the kids have been placed first in one school and then in the other. The mother is very shallow. She says that she is interested in her children, but after talking with her, it is obvious that she has very little concern for them and lets them fend for themselves. She seems to get real pleasure from LaDonna's acting out, and corrects her only in the presence of school officials. She has not been cooperative with the school in any way, and places the blame for the situation outside of herself and her children. She operates on the pleasure principle and sets quite marginal standards for the youngsters and herself.

⊷⊷⊷⊷

A final group consists of low-choice children who displayed seriously disturbed behavior. Some of this behavior is disruptive of the normal operation of the classroom. Earlier work in this program with child guidance clinic cases indicated that if a child seemed seriously disturbed to a psychiatrist, he almost invariably also seemed disturbed to his classmates and to the teacher. Another finding here is also in line with child guidance clinic experience. There, the ratio of boys to girls is at least four or five to one. Here, too, it is more difficult to find girls than boys who exhibit disturbed, acting-out behavior. Another thing to be noticed in this group is that the frequency of bizarre or really disturbed parents is greater than in the groups of better adjusted children presented earlier. It should also be mentioned that the children in this group are from various socioeconomic levels. Finally, some of these pupils show how deviant behavior can be in the most extreme cases present in a classroom situation.

Rudy (fourth grade) looks like an average sized fourth-grader, but he is two years overage. He appears rather happy and carefree, but he is a disturbed boy. His pants sag and his sleeves come down over his hands. His jackets are usually ragged looking. He has been wearing an old Army hat lately.

Rudy's pleasant disposition makes a good first impression, but he forms no lasting friendships. He has been seeking the favor of a boy in his room who has serious emotional problems. Rudy has attended six schools and lived at ten different addresses during the last six years. He talks a blue streak and many of his tales are pure fantasy. He shows enthusiasm for history and fiction, but getting him to work is a hopeless task. He is restless and overactive and bothers the children around him. Rudy wants to be liked and he responds to attention and praise. He is never openly defiant but he does not respond to criticism; nothing seems to faze him. He spends his time copying poems and reading books instead of doing his work. Rudy talks with authority on any subject, and sometimes surprises the teacher and classmates with his detailed information. Mostly he rambles on with irrelevant thoughts. He makes a nuisance of himself during the noon hour and needs constant supervision.

On the playground, Rudy annoys other children but is never mean or bullying. He makes himself known inside the classroom or out by pushing and shoving others and using vulgar language. His classmates frequently complain about him. Last year Rudy was expelled from school because his behavior was considered intolerable. His present teacher has given up trying to make him work. Rudy is good in rhythms, enjoys gym, but his enthusiasm is poorly controlled. He seems fearful and rather cowardly, often hiding from the children he has antagonized. He walks home from school with his seven-year-old brother. He frequently complains that the children want to beat up on him.

Rudy has had psychological and psychiatric studies. Placement outside his home has been recommended. Rudy is an anxious and confused boy who hasn't learned the social values others take for granted. He doesn't seem to be aware that he has problems.

Rudy is the oldest of four children. The father is not in the home, and the mother is on welfare. She is known for her peculiarities. She claims to be an ex–circus strongwoman and a faith healer. Both the mother and Rudy are receiving extensive social casework services. Plans are under way to place him in a boarding home on a temporary basis. The younger brother has fewer emotional problems and his classroom behavior is more acceptable. There seems to be little consistency in the mother's treatment of her children, changing from overprotection to neglect. When Rudy was in the lower grades of school, his mother often dressed him in girls' clothing, frilly blouses and underwear. The mother is interested in reading, and there is a wealth of paperback books in the home. The school has had poor cooperation from the mother.

≈≈≈≈≈≈

Martha (fifth grade) is a large, rather pretty girl who is a little heavy but usually neat and tidy. She is a mentally disturbed child who was in a special class last year, but came back to regular school this year. The special class placement was made because of "extreme physical quarrelsomeness, crying, fighting, etc." She is very lovable this year compared to the year before last, but still very erratic in behavior. She is extremely kind, considerate and helpful in her better moods, and is very fond of little children. Scholastically, she is average but has a short attention span. Her assignments must be very specific. She is a year older than the other children since she repeated fourth grade at the special school. Martha has a real need for someone to talk to. The school librarian has taken her on as a helper, and she seems to be enjoying and profiting from the extra attention.

On the playground, Martha's behavior seems pretty normal. She gets along reasonably well except on her bad days. She likes to be part of other children's activities and wants to be chosen and play games with them. Early in the year she was thoroughly un-accepted by the other children. The patrols were constantly report-ing her. The teacher has told the other children a little about Martha's problems, and they seem to be trying to help her.

In the classroom her behavior is essentially normal, although she is rather talkative with her neighbors. She is a restless child who has a hard time staying busy. She is very pleasant to the teacher. Even at her worst she is very polite and can always be reasoned with.

Her present low standing with her peers is probably temporary in that she has been in one of her most belligerent moods. Her behavior is erratic, but was fairly good until this spring (apparently following a pattern set in previous years). In spring her behavior gets very bad and usually ends in some physical illness. When she returns to school her behavior improves. The year before her special class placement she would run out of her room into another class-room yelling, pick fights in the cloakroom, and so forth.

The mother has been very cooperative and the home situation at present seems to be a good one.

∞∞∞∞∞

The teacher laughed mirthlessly when Mac (fifth grade) was mentioned as the subject of her first interview. He is extremely good looking. His dress, however, is erratic. He was expelled last week. He had been in school for only a small part of the day, since he went to a special reading class. He is thought to have some brain damage. Although he has average intelligence, he is extremely stub-born and defiant and often gets violent. He has struck the teacher, and the week he has been gone has been terrific for her. He is like a split personality. He can be extremely charming on his good days. He seems to crave attention and will ask for it, he seems pleased momentarily to get it and then suddenly turns on you. Academically, he has done absolutely nothing all year. He works only when he feels like it. He did work very hard on a story for his special reading teacher. This was filled with death and violence.

On the playground, Mac gets into trouble constantly. At the beginning of the year he had the children buffaloed in fear of him. Then he was beaten up by a smaller child, so now he is afraid of the other children. When others are playing games, Mac pushes his way in. The teacher has had to prevent him from doing serious injury to others by kicking at their vulnerable places.

His behavior in the building depends on his mood in the morn-ing. If he is happy and the teacher ignores him, he will sit for hours and not do a thing. However, if she expects him to do anything, he becomes very belligerent, violent, will try to kick down the door, and so on. The teacher has had to have him bodily ejected by a man. He once kicked a little girl in the chest for no reason. The principal says that if Mac says "Good morning" to him, he knows he won't be sent down to his office that day; but if he rushes by him or ignores him he knows there will be trouble. Mac seems to feel inadequate in relation to the other students. He is a perfectionist and can't get any writing completed because every letter must be just so. His motor coordination seems to be affected by the brain damage, so that writing is very slow for him. He is always saying that he can do the work, but that he doesn't want to. His behavior with the teacher has been up and down. At first he seemed to like the teacher very much. She tried not to ask him for very much. But when she pressured him to perform, the antagonism started coming out, and he has been getting progressively worse. His behavior is extremely variable from bad to good. He forgets quickly and doesn't seem to hold a grudge from one day to the next. The other students have gotten used to the fact that he is bound to get in trouble. The better students ignore him. Some children want to help him.

His is a strict–not strict family. The father is a rigid "religious fanatic" whose entire family is terrified of him. He demands too much, but gets nothing. The mother is a very inadequate person; she kowtows to the father and doesn't stick up for the children. It is an old-fashioned home; the father is lord and master. This boy is currently undergoing psychiatric treatment.

∞∞∞∞∞

Mark (sixth grade) is a short, stocky, average-looking boy who is healthy and quite handsome, with dark hair and skin. He is always clean and is clothes conscious. When he wants to smile he has a very appealing expression. He has some definite enthusiasms which seem to be increasing. However, he is constantly in trouble, has a need to get attention in negative ways, and for a number of years has been one of the worst behavior problems in school.

Mark likes games, but cheats as much as he can. He is a bully, wanting to be in control and to have his own way. He is a disturbing element in class; he tries to get others' attention away from their work, but pays little attention himself. He daydreams much of the time, even when he is looking directly at his book. He is resentful when admonished by the teacher. When he is in some kind of trouble he will laugh nervously, almost impulsively, with rapid convulsive-like movements. This action, which others think of as laughter, is an almost uncontrollable hysterical reaction. During the past year or two he has at times been almost threatening toward the teachers. Mark has recently been put on probation for his misbehavior outside of school, and he has been going to a child guidance clinic.

During the past few weeks his relationship to the other children, particularly the boys, seems improved. For the first time he has been invited to birthday parties, and for the first time he has been known to do things for the children. On his own birthday he brought small presents for the whole class.

Previously, when Mark was in trouble others usually reacted by laughing and giving him the attention he seemed to want. Recently they were asked not to do this. Now they are more apt to ignore him, and he is no longer able to get attention. For the first time this year he has been readmitted into gym class, where, so far, he has been getting along well.

Mark comes from a broken home. There has been serious conflict between his parents, and they are working out a divorce. The father had to be kept away from the home by a restraining order. The mother has been unwilling to work with the school on Mark's problems, and has been generally antagonistic toward the school, though she has called the principal many times to discuss her problems. The father felt the mother was neglecting Mark, but he has not been willing to bring this up in court. The home situation has been very unhappy for Mark, an only child, for many years.

≈≈≈≈≈

Frank (fourth grade) is a tall, thin, nice-looking boy with brown hair and eyes. He is clean and neat. He feels alone and tries to make friends, but his overtures are rejected by his classmates. Frank has unusually good manners and is always considerate and very polite to his teacher. He is emotionally unstable and has had several outbursts which indicate psychotic tendencies. He has nervous mannerisms. It appears that he is almost completely lacking in self-control if he is needled by another child. He is interested in sports, but can't seem to enter into group activities. He frequently kicks and has injured two girls quite seriously within the last month.

The children reject him. Frank is frequently irritable, restless, hyperactive, and insolent. He swears frequently on the playground and on several occasions has used the most obscene language. If chided by certain students, he becomes surly and tense. Some children seem to irritate him more than others. Frank has always accepted discipline from his teacher. He is always considerate and polite to her. However, the teacher has observed his explosive reaction when he retaliated against another student. It took Frank half an hour to blow off steam and regain composure. One day he had trouble with a certain boy, but had probably been needled by this boy all year. When Frank reached the saturation point, he whipped off his belt and started to beat the other child. After this action was stopped, Frank spent much time giving a tongue lashing to his victim and in berating all of the people he hated. He hated quite a few people too. Frank, as one might suspect, has trouble concentrating. He also has less aptitude for independent work than the other pupils in the room.

Frank has had a very unstable family life. He and his sixth-grade sister and mother moved into this school district last September. Frank's father is dead and his mother was released recently from a state mental hospital. She is a very bright woman, but completely unstable. She has been described as paranoid. She has been vindictive in her criticism of the principal and teacher. She makes bizarre requests of the school and has a ridiculous imagination about what goes on in the school and on the playground. Her request for custody of the children has been denied, so that the county has custody of them for an additional six months. The family has moved about six times this past year; however, they have remained in the same school district. This extreme instability and the lack of psychiatric treatment for the mother is affecting Frank. The school is very concerned about this family.

3

~~~~~~

Intercorrelations of
Measures, Cross-Sectional
and Over Time

INTERCORRELATIONS OF SCORES

It has long been known to those studying peer status that negative
choices or scores are not the exact opposite of positive choices or scores.
The positive and negative choice scores correlate about $+.50$ (when
the LL scores have been reversed so that the greatest number of choices
gets the lowest score). This less than perfect inverse correlation between positive and negative peer status indices means that these scores
have somewhat different meanings. A complete absence of positive
choices does not indicate whether the person involved is overlooked or
actively rejected by the group. However, because of their definite relationship, these have been combined into an LM – LL score which has
a much more symmetric distribution than either the LM or LL scores
by themselves. In the grade school situation, where the teachers have
the same pupils in class most of the day, it is possible to get Teacher
Ratings of peer status which are highly meaningful. These were obtained for all pupils; the extent to which they correlate with the pupils'
nominations will be indicated below.

The cross-sectional correlations to be presented here are based on
the 34,366 first-year pupils for whom we had complete sets of scores
(both LM and LL peer choice scores and TR). The correlations of the
first-year peer scores (LM with LL; LM with TR; LL with TR; and LM – LL
with TR) are shown in Table 4 for the total sample, and for breakdowns
by sex, grade, state, and SES. For the total sample the LM scores, based

on four choices, correlated more highly (.53) with the TR than did the LL based on two choices by each child. This is in line with almost all

Table 4. Intercorrelations of First-Year Peer Scores by Sex, Grade, State, and SES

Category and Number	LM, LL	LM, TR	LL, TR	(LM − LL), TR
Total (N = 34,366)	.50	.53	.45	.57
By sex				
Boys (N = 17,559)	.48	.52	.45	.57
Girls (N = 16,807)	.51	.53	.44	.57
By grade				
Third (N = 8,441)	.50	.53	.45	.57
Fourth (N = 8,754)	.49	.53	.45	.57
Fifth (N = 8,363)	.50	.53	.45	.57
Sixth (N = 8,808)	.50	.52	.44	.56
By state				
Minnesota (N = 17,075)	.47	.54	.46	.58
Texas (N = 17,291)	.52	.51	.44	.55
By ses (one Minnesota city only)				
I (N = 2,926)	.51	.57	.51	.62
II (N = 2,956)	.46	.53	.47	.59
III (N = 2,783)	.49	.54	.52	.61
IV (N = 2,880)	.48	.53	.46	.58

the other experience of this study. The somewhat higher correlation of the composite LM − LL with TR (.57) is about what would be expected.

The differences between the two sexes in these cross-sectional correlations are too small to deserve discussion. The correlations for boys and for girls of LM − LL with TR are identical, .57. Whether or not there is a systematic change in these correlations at different grade levels is also a matter of definite interest. The answer again is that there is no evidence of a trend large enough to merit discussion.

The correlation of LM with LL scores is slightly higher for the Texas sample than for the Minnesota sample. The correlations of TR with the three peer scores are slightly higher in Minnesota.

The breakdown by SES is given only for the total public school population of one Minnesota city (see also p. 67 below). These results give no support at all to the idea that the lower-class pupil is so far beyond the comprehension of the middle-class teacher as to make the whole educational enterprise ineffectual in the school setting.

It is possible that annual testing over several years could have some cumulative effect on the results after the first test administration. To investigate this, correlations were computed for all those pupils with complete scores at the sixth-grade level in three consecutive years.

These results are shown in the accompanying tabulation. Here the pupils and teachers in the first year would have had only one test administration, in the second year most would have had two administrations, and so on. Inspection of this set of correlations indicates no consistent trend with the passage of years. There is no indication that the repeated testing had any appreciable effect on the results.

	1st Year *(N = 8,808)*	*2nd Year* *(N = 3,978)*	*3rd Year* *(N = 2,684)*
LM vs. LL	.50	.51	.50
LM vs. TR	.52	.54	.56
LL vs. TR	.44	.38	.41
(LM − LL) vs. TR	.56	.54	.57

The correlations between the components of various combined scores and these combined scores are, of course, very high because the composite is made up of the obtained scores. Since any variation of these from one group to another would be a direct function of variations in the component scores, and since Table 4 and the tabulation above showed no consistent trends in various breakdowns, these correlations of obtained scores with LM − LL and peer-teacher combined scores are shown for the first-year total sample only in the accompanying tabulation.

	Correlation (N = 34,366)
LM/LM − LL	.89
LL/LM − LL	.83
LM/[2(LM − LL) + TR]	.86
LL/[2(LM − LL) + TR]	.78
LM − LL/[2(LM − LL) + TR]	.96
TR/[2(LM − LL) + TR]	.76

It may be remembered that the combined peer-teacher rating score was computed by the formula $2(LM - LL) + TR$. The correlation of LM − LL (.96) with this combined score is very high, and the correlation of TR with the combined score is lower, as expected (.76). In spite of the size of these correlations, there are some detectable differences in the size of the correlations of the peer-teacher combined score with other variables when compared with those of LM and LL taken alone or together. As will be shown in the next section, the peer-teacher combined score is slightly more stable over time than the LM − LL score by itself.

59

THE JUNIOR HIGH SCHOOL SAMPLE

The main study is concerned with the peer status and related characteristics of elementary school children in the third through sixth grades. This interval was defined at the lower age by the ability of the pupils to follow the prescribed procedures adequately. It was defined at the upper age by the end of the grade school period, which marked a change from a situation in which the same teacher had the same children all day to one where the children had different teachers for different subjects.

What these pupils were like in subsequent years was obviously a matter of substantial interest. In Texas where some of the participating cities were not large, administration of the peer choice procedures was continued in some places through the seventh, eighth, and ninth grades. In Minnesota, on the other hand, where the two cities were large, and each junior high school draws students from several grade schools, no attempt was made to obtain peer choices at junior high school level, since the situation differed greatly from that at the grade school level.

The results obtained from the junior high school sample in Texas are presented here in one place, although the information presented spreads over several chapters for the main grade school group. Comparison of the results given here can be made by turning to the appropriate chapter.

The intercorrelations of peer scores obtained during the third year of the study are shown in Table 5 for the seventh and eighth grades, together and separately, and for boys and girls. For the entire group, these correlations are consistently lower than those for the entire third- through sixth-grade group. There are no marked and

Table 5. Junior High Intercorrelations of Third-Year Peer Scores by Sex and Grade, Texas Only

Category and Number	LM, LL	LM, TR	LL, TR	(LM − LL), TR
Total (N = 1,652)	.47	.48	.31	.47
By sex				
Boys (N = 851)	.43	.46	.29	.45
Girls (N = 801)	.52	.51	.34	.49
By grade				
Seventh (N = 856)	.47	.46	.30	.44
Eighth (N = 796)	.48	.51	.33	.50

consistent differences between the seventh and eighth grade correlations; this is in line with results for the earlier grades. The intercorrelations for girls are slightly higher than those for boys. This is not the same as the results from the lower grades, but the differences are not large.

The stability coefficients for different scores are shown in Table 6 for one-, two-, and three-year intervals. Those coefficients which have

Table 6. Stability Coefficients for Peer Choice and Teacher Rating Scores between Test and Retest of Junior High Group, Texas Only ($N = 95$)

Interval between Tests and Grades Compared	LM	LL	LM − LL	TR	(LM − LL)/TR
One-year interval					
Grade 6 vs. 7	.38	.48	.49	.32	.48
Grade 7 vs. 8	.16	.48	.38	.18	.33
Grade 8 vs. 9	.29	.36	.39	.23	.41
Two-year interval					
Grade 6 vs. 8	.35	.34	.34	.23	.40
Grade 7 vs. 9	.21	.29	.30	.35	.30
Three-year interval: Grade 6 vs. 9 ...	.24	.39	.39	.35	.38

the sixth grade as the lower year run higher than those in which the initial year is the seventh or eighth grade. This is definitely so for the one- and two-year intervals. For the three-year interval, sixth to ninth grade, the coefficients are about as high as for the one-year interval, eighth to ninth grade. The sixth-grade scores are somewhat more stable than the later ones, when they are paired with the different junior high school years. This indicates that it is the stability of the sixth-grade scores, rather than shifts during the junior high school period, which are important in producing this effect.

STABILITY AND CHANGE
IN SCORES OVER TIME

The plan of the study called for large-scale initial administration of the peer choice and teacher ratings and the obtaining of longitudinal scores annually until those who had begun in third grade completed the sixth grade. In the Texas groups followed into junior high school, the pupils in the sixth grade at the time of first testing had reached the ninth grade at the time of final testing.

In a very large-scale project of this kind, which involves the cooperation of, and interaction with, a variety of school systems, it is not possible to set down a rigid plan which can be closely adhered to. Some shifts have to be made in accordance with the willingness of the participants to continue and for other reasons. There were inevitably some unscheduled changes in teachers which interfered with the plan to get ratings made by teachers who knew the children well. For example, one teacher broke her leg while skiing just before the study began.

Thus, data were available for the original sample, for a markedly smaller sample with scores on two successive years, and for gradually smaller samples extending over three- and four-year intervals. Results are presented here for the two-year longitudinal sample, which includes all those for whom scores were available for both the first and the second years. The longitudinal samples shrank because some pupils moved out of their school districts, the number of participating cities dropped, and pupils who moved into a school district after the first testing were not included. Correlations between scores on each yearly measure and scores on the same measure in subsequent years can be considered indicators of the stability of each measure.

Stability Coefficients over One Year. The correlation between scores obtained during spring of the third-grade year and the scores obtained for the same children in the spring of the fourth-grade year are shown in Table 7. The correlations over a one-year interval also permit a comparison of the correlations obtained when the teacher and many of the classmates would have changed. These correlations can, of course, include only those pupils present both years. One methodological question of interest was what would happen to these one-

Table 7. Stability Coefficients for Peer Choice and Teacher Rating Scores with One-Year Interval between Test and Retest

| Score | Total Group | | 2-Year Sample | | 2-Year Sample | |
	2-Year Sample	4-Year Sample	Boys	Girls	Texas	Minn.
LM	.52	.52	.49	.55	.48	.54
LL	.36	.38	.31	.41	.38	.34
LM − LL	.52	.53	.51	.53	.50	.54
TR	.47	.46	.40	.54	.42	.51
2(LM − LL)/TR	.58	.59	.53	.63	.54	.61
N	1,545	1,156	780	765	635	910

year stability correlations when they were obtained on the sample present in the first two years of the study, as compared with those which would be obtained when this shrinkage from pupils' moving out had occurred over a longer period. To make this comparison, one-year stability correlations were computed both for the second-year longitudinal sample ($N = 1,545$) and for the fourth-year longitudinal sample, consisting of those present in all four years of the study ($N = 1,156$).

Both these second- and fourth-year sample correlations are presented in Table 7 for the total group of the two states combined. There is not enough difference between the two sets of correlations to deserve comment. Table 7 also presents the one-year interval correlations for boys compared with girls and for Texas compared with Minnesota.

For both the second- and fourth-year samples, the LM scores are noticeably more stable than the LL scores. The combined LM – LL score is only slightly more stable than the LM score by itself. Stability of TR scores is intermediate between that for LL and LM scores. As would be expected, the composite peer-teacher score is the most stable.

A second interesting problem concerns the comparison of the stability of boys' and girls' scores. The one-year stability coefficients are somewhat higher for girls than for boys. The LM scores and the LL scores are somewhat more stable for girls than for boys. TR scores for girls also vary less from one year to another than the rating scores for boys. This greater stability of girls' TR scores is interesting in view of the fact that teacher accuracy (the correlation score between TR and LM – LL) is no greater for girls than for boys (p. 67).

Part of the basic strategy of the project was the simultaneous replication of the study in the two states of Texas and Minnesota. Except for the LL scores, the stability coefficients are a little higher for Minnesota than for Texas.

Stability Coefficients with One-Year Interval and Rising Grade Level. Another set of stability coefficients that will add to the picture is that consisting of the one-year correlations with the largest possible samples for third to fourth, fourth to fifth, and fifth to sixth grades. Inspections of these will show whether the drop in correlations from the third to sixth grade as compared with those for shorter intervals is due to the interval or is due to a change in the correlations from one grade to another over a one-year period. These values are shown in the accompanying tabulation for both states combined. The N's vary because each grade comparison included different children. Neither the LM nor the LL correlations show a consistent trend with a rise in grade levels. The same is true for the TR and the combined peer-teacher scores. There is no indication of any marked and consistent change from the third- to fourth-year correlations through the fifth- to sixth-year correlations. Thus, the changes discussed below for longer time intervals are due to the interval rather than to the rise in grade level.

	Grade 3 vs. 4	Grade 4 vs. 5	Grade 5 vs. 6
LM	.56	.58	.53
LL	.44	.46	.46
LM − LL	.58	.60	.56
TR	.48	.46	.45
2(LM − LL) + TR	.62	.65	.61

One-, Two-, and Three-Year Stability Coefficients. In making a comparison between stability coefficients over one, two, and three years, the four-year longitudinal sample was employed, so that the correlations are based on the same children. This means that the correlations from year to year were based on a total group of 1,156 rather than the 2,785 for which one-year stability coefficients were presented above. It has been shown that the inclusion or exclusion of children who moved out of these schools had little effect on the stability coefficients, but the restriction to the four-year longitudinal sample ensures rigor in the comparison of correlations over various lengths of time.

Stability coefficients for the total four-year sample in both states are shown in Table 8 for the same children at one-, two-, and three-year intervals, for the basic peer choice scores, for Teacher Ratings, and for the composite score. The normal expectation here is that the correlations would drop slightly with each additional year between tests and retests. For the LM scores (based on four choices by each pupil) the correlation drops from .52 over a one-year interval to .42 over three years. The LL scores (based on only two choices by each pupil) show less correlation over the one-year interval but decline less as the interval increases to three years. The LM − LL correlations are slightly higher than those for LM alone, and reflect the fact that they are a combination of the two other scores. The TR coefficients show less change in stability from one to three years than do the LM scores. The composite peer-teacher scores show the greatest stability of all and change as they would be expected to do from the behavior of their component scores.

In general, the changes shown here are similar in pattern to longitudinal scores obtained from intelligence tests, or in the correlation between learning trials where there is a progressive drop with increasing distance between the trials.

Table 8. Stability Coefficients for Peer Choice and Teacher Rating
Scores for One-, Two-, and Three-Year Intervals

Interval between Tests	LM	LL	LM − LL	TR	2(LM − LL) + TR
One-year interval (grade 3 vs. 4)					
Combined[a] .... .52		.38	.53	.46	.59
Boys[b] .... .50		.31	.49	.39	.54
Girls[c] .... .53		.44	.57	.53	.63
Two-year interval (grade 3 vs. 5)					
Combined[a] .... .47		.35	.48	.44	.55
Boys[b] .... .43		.35	.47	.35	.52
Girls[c] .... .50		.34	.49	.50	.57
Three-year interval (grade 3 vs. 6)					
Combined[a] .... .42		.34	.45	.43	.52
Boys[b] .... .39		.34	.41	.36	.46
Girls[c] .... .45		.34	.48	.50	.57

[a]$N = 1,156$ boys and girls in both states.
[b]$N = 566$ in both states.
[c]$N = 590$ in both states.

A comparison of stability scores for this same sample broken down by sex is also shown in Table 8. For the LM scores, stability for girls is somewhat greater than that for boys for all three intervals. For LL scores, this is true for the one-year, but not for the two- and three-year intervals. The TR show markedly greater stability for girls than for boys, but as has been shown elsewhere, this greater stability is not associated with greater accuracy of rating when compared with pupil choice. The composite peer-teacher scores reflect a greater stability for girls in the other scores.

Comparison of the stability coefficient four-year sample in Texas as compared with the four-year sample in Minnesota is given in Appendix Table 2. In comparison with the stability obtainable with some of our larger samples, correlations based on small samples of these sizes tend to be less stable. For the LM score, the stability coefficient is somewhat higher for Minnesota than for Texas, but this difference has essentially vanished in the three-year correlations. For the LL scores there is little difference between the two states. Both the correlations for TR are slightly higher for Minnesota at all three intervals, but the initial difference in the correlations for the composite peer-teacher scores vanishes at the three-year level.

Stability Coefficients in Relationship to Socioeconomic Status. Stability coefficients in relation to SES are available (Appendix Table 2) only for the second Minnesota city, for the third and fourth quartiles in SES. For the LM scores the initially larger stability coefficient for SES III over one year changed to essentially the same size over a three-year interval. For the LL scores there is a possibility of error in the SES III one-year interval score, where a separate breakdown for this group by choices and girls shows that the correlation for boys is enough lower than all the other coefficients in that row to be suspect. For the LL scores over a three-year interval there is no difference at all between the SES III and IV stability coefficients. The year-to-year Teacher Rating coefficients run a little higher at all three intervals for SES III. This differs from the finding on a much larger sample that there is no difference in teacher accuracy (cross-sectional) at these two SES levels. The stability coefficient for the composite peer-teacher scores again converges at the three-year interval. Whether or not this convergence of stability coefficients with increase in interval has any real meaning is not known to us. It would be interesting to see whether anything like this has occurred with other kinds of longitudinal data.

TEACHER RATINGS
AND TEACHERS' ACCURACY

Since it may sometimes be easier to obtain teacher ratings than peer choices for groups of children, it seemed desirable to explore thoroughly the problem of the relation between teacher ratings of peer status and the children's peer choices. This relation will be referred to as an indication of teacher accuracy, with the children's choices as criteria.

The teachers were asked not whether or not they liked the children, but rather how well the other children liked each child in turn (the specific instructions are given in Appendix A). The teacher ratings were turned in when the numbered rosters were sent in for duplication, before peer choices were made. The teacher ratings were, of course, influenced by the frequent informal choosing situations which occur in the normal course of classroom and playground activities which sometimes led a teacher to observe that a child is "always the last one chosen." Teacher ratings were obtained for almost every child in the study. Because of the large total sample, there was an unusual amount of stability in the TR correlations. These are given in Table 9 for various breakdowns.

The first relationships presented here are those between TR and peer choices for the total sample and for the third, fourth, fifth, and sixth grades separately (Table 9). It can be seen that these are identi-

Table 9. Teacher Accuracy: Correlations between Teacher Ratings and Peer Status Scores

Category	N	Correlation of TR vs. (LM − LL)
Total sample	34,366	.57
By grade		
Third	8,441	.57
Fourth	8,754	.57
Fifth	8,363	.57
Sixth	8,808	.56
By sex		
Boys	17,559	.57
Girls	16,807	.57
By state		
Texas	17,291	.55
Minnesota	17,075	.58
By SES (Minnesota only)		
I	2,926	.62
II	2,959	.59
III	2,783	.61
IV	2,880	.58

cal for the first three grades and only .01 lower for the sixth grade. The accuracy of TR is essentially identical at all four grade levels. The correlations are somewhat higher than those reported by Gage, Leavitt, and Stone (1955), who compared the judgments of 103 fourth-, fifth-, and sixth-grade teachers with the results of a sociometric test administered to their pupils. An average teacher-pupil correlation of .48 was obtained.

The total sample of pupils is approximately evenly divided between girls and boys, with a slightly greater number of boys. (The number of female teachers is much greater than the number of male teachers; a teacher comparison by sex is given below.) It can be seen from Table 9 that there is no difference at all in the teacher accuracy of rating girls and of rating boys. This is in line with Gronlund (1950a&b) and Gronlund and Algard (1958).

Results of these comparisons of teacher accuracy by grade level and by sex did not differ markedly from information already in the literature. In several other areas important to the plan of this study we were unable to find anything in the earlier literature close enough to our procedures to make such comparisons possible. We found no study where the same procedure was applied in states in two different parts of the country. In general, similar results would be expected with large samples of children from two different areas, but there is nothing at all in the general procedures of statistical inference which indicates that this has to be the case.

A comparison of Teacher Ratings with peer choices by state is also given in Table 9. Although the correlation is slightly higher in the Minnesota sample and the difference is non-chance, it is not large enough to encourage the formation of hypotheses about reasons why it may have occurred.

There has been a great deal of discussion about the problem of the middle-class teacher and the lower-class pupil. Much of this has insisted that socioeconomic class (and the occasionally correlated racial) differences between teacher and pupil are so profound that there can be no effective interaction between them. If this were so, a much higher correlation would be expected between the ratings by middle-class teachers and the peer choices among middle-class children than would be the case in schools of low SES, since the teacher would be well able to comprehend the child of his or her own middle-class background but so unable to understand lower-class children that any agreement between teacher rating and peer choices would be purely coincidental. That this is simply not so is indicated by the correlations in Table 9. In the Minnesota city where all four SES quartiles are represented, there is no consistent trend up or down the SES scale. In the two lower quartiles of the other Minnesota city, the difference between the peer score correlations in the lower-middle quartile and the lowest quartile is .01. The teachers in this study were well able to comprehend the social structure of their classes at all SES levels. Insofar as agreement between teacher rating and pupil choices indicates an awareness by teachers of the feelings of their pupils, there is simply no difference across socioeconomic levels which would support theories dealing with lack of comprehension of lower-class pupils by teachers with middle-class backgrounds. It is possible that there are locations where different results would be obtained, but these are the results that appeared here.

One aspect of the accuracy problem of teacher ratings which has received some attention is the problem of individual differences in ability to rate other persons. For example, Gronlund (1950) reported that in forty classes of sixth-grade students, "There is a difference between teachers in the accuracy of each teacher's judgments of the sociometric status of sixth-grade pupils in the classroom. Correlation coefficients representing the average accuracy of each teacher's judgments ranged from .268 to .838 with a mean of .595." In this context, any attempt to appraise the skill of a set of raters must inevitably pay some attention to what is being rated. This may be illustrated very simply by a comparison of line lengths.

A ——— ———   B ——— ——

If we have two pairs of lines, pair A being almost exactly the same length and pair B differing markedly in length, the amount of agreement between successive ratings by the same individual (or also between different raters) would be much greater for ratings of the length of the two lines of pair B than they would be for the length of the two lines of pair A. Applying this same reasoning to classes of twenty-five or thirty students, it would not be possible to get a meaningful measure of the rating skill of an individual in relation to a class unless you knew whether this class consisted mainly of pupils who did not differ much (as in pair A of the lines) or contained some individuals who were obviously above or below the others (as in pair B).

Previous discussions of TR in relation to grade, sex, and so forth have implicitly assumed that with a large number of classes, the ratability of classes would even out. However, when we attempt to appraise the rating skill of an individual teacher based on the one class he or she knows well enough to rate, it is almost impossible to get meaningful results in the absence of information about the dispersion of scores in the class being rated. In other words, if the class is more similar to the pair A situation, any teacher would have some difficulty in rating them. If some members of the class are similar to pair B, almost any teacher who knew the children could rate them fairly accurately.

A year-to-year teacher accuracy analysis was made based on *all* teachers in the second Minnesota city who participated in both the first- and second-year studies; there were 115. Correlations were computed between TR and pupil peer choices in each of these two years; then rank-difference correlations were computed between the teachers' correlations in the first year and the same teachers' correlations in the second year. These values are as follows: the accuracy of ratings of boys, first versus second year, is .12; the accuracy of ratings of girls, first

	Correlation
Male teachers (N = 72)	+.09
Female teachers (N = 156)	+.06
Male and female combined (N = 228)	+.07

versus second year, is .13. It can be seen that there is little relation between teacher accuracy in the two years. These correlations, though positive, are so small that they would be of little practical value in determining that one teacher can rate more accurately than another, or that accuracy in judging peer status is an important variable as a characteristic of teachers.

A further indication that teacher accuracy is unsatisfactory as a postulated characteristic of individual teachers is given by the relation between teachers' accuracy in rating boys and their accuracy in rating girls in the same class. Correlations are presented in the accompanying tabulation for male and female teachers for the second Minnesota city. These correlations are based on data for the first and second years, so that the class rather than the teacher is the unit to which the N's apply. It can be seen that all correlations are very small and that correlations are almost identical for male and female teachers.

The four-year longitudinal sample was studied to determine the accuracy of teacher ratings in the first year (third grade) compared with peer ratings one, two, and three years later in the fourth, fifth, and sixth grades. The TR for one year in comparison with the peer ratings (LM − LL) one year later correlate .40, somewhat lower than the .56 obtained when the teacher rated the same class on which the peer scores were being obtained. There is substantial stability in this correlation against the third- and fourth-year peer ratings. Once the change is made from the situation in which the teacher is rating the class making peer choices to the situation in which the children have progressed to different classrooms, the year-to-year change in correlations of first-year TR with later peer choices is not marked (see Table 10).

Table 10. First-Year Teacher Ratings in Relation to Subsequent Peer Status (N = 1,156)

Year and Grade	TR (1st Yr) and LM	TR (1st Yr) and LL	TR (1st Yr) and LM − LL
First year (grade 3 vs. 3)	.54	.38	.56
Second year (grade 3 vs. 4)	.39	.29	.40
Third year (grade 3 vs. 5)	.36	.28	.37
Fourth year (grade 3 vs. 6)	.32	.28	.34

The correlation of TR for LL scores is markedly lower than those for LM. It might be inferred from this that the teachers were less able to identify the less-liked children than the more-liked children; however, the LL scores compared with the LM scores have been consistently lower in every comparison except that of split-half reliability coefficients. In other words, the LL correlations are lower from one year to another for peer choices as well as for TR.

It is very important to get as accurate a picture as possible of the effectiveness of teacher ratings, since these are more easily obtainable than pupil choices and can be used as a substitute for them. The agreement between teachers and pupil ratings is at least as good as that between teachers and measured IQ.

The fact that teachers at different socioeconomic levels were about equally effective in rating their children strongly suggests that statements about the gap between the middle-class teacher and the lower-class child needs to be defined and supported by factual evidence, rather than assumed inevitably to be present.

The finding that there is a lack of correlation between teachers' ratings made in one year with ratings made in a second year on a completely different classroom indicates the difficulty or impossibility of measuring "teachers' accuracy" in terms of a single class. Until this has been appraised on more than one class, such a measure must be regarded as definitely tentative in nature.

4

~~~~~~

Various Factors
Relating to Peer Status

RELATIONS BETWEEN THE PEER STATUS
OF CHOOSER AND CHOSEN

The central problem of this chapter concerns the relations between
the peer status of children making choices and the peer status of the
children they choose, on positive choices, negative choices, and a combination of a positive and negative choice. In terms of the research
literature, this information relates to two somewhat different areas.
The first of these is the somewhat heterogeneous set of reports having
to do in one way or another with the perception of others. The second
bears on the more technical problem of the use of matrices in deriving
basic choice scores.

Social Perception Studies. "Social perception" includes studies of
"accuracy of social perception," "the understanding of others," "the
ability to forecast others' sociometric status," "group relevant social
perception," and the relationship of any of these or related concepts to
"effectiveness in interpersonal relationships" insofar as this is related
to choice status. One "finding" that has sometimes been reported in
work of this kind is that in a choice situation people tend to choose
"upward." Since the highly chosen are by definition those who receive
more choices than others, it would seem inevitable that they would
receive more than their share of choices from those with lower scores.
This would hardly seem to need empirical illustration.

Social perception studies can be divided for convenience into three

73

types. Type one deals with the relationship between choice status of choosers and their predictions of the choice status of others, and includes studies of the relationship between choice status and accuracy of prediction of peers' response to a standard psychological inventory or questionnaire, or between choice status and ability to predict the choice status of others in the group. With a wide variety of samples and considerable variations in procedures, some investigators have found a positive correlation between perceiving or judging others' status or responses and *own* actual status (Gage, 1952; Goslin, 1962; Green, 1948; Gronlund, 1955; Lewis & Spilka, 1960). On the other hand Ausubel, in a series of studies, found no such relationship (Ausubel, 1953; Ausubel & Schiff, 1955). The possibility of a qualified relationship, in which the correlation between chooser's own status and his predictions for others depends on circumstances, also exists (Exline, 1960).

Type two studies relate the individual's choice status to his estimate that a certain *number* of other individuals would choose him. Again under varied conditions, a positive relationship between *own* perceived or judged status and *own* actual status has been reported by a variety of investigators (Ausubel, 1955; Ausubel & Schiff, 1955; Gallagher, 1958; Goslin, 1962; Gronlund, 1955; O'Connor, 1960; Trent, 1959). These indicate that persons tend to have awareness of their own peer status.

Type three studies may be defined as including those comparing leaders with non-leaders in accuracy of appraisal of group opinion on some topic or topics. Leaders were found to be superior in appraising group opinions in some studies (Bell & Hall, 1954; Chowdhry & Newcomb, 1952; Greer, Galanter, & Nordlie, 1954). On the other hand, little or no relationship was found by others (Cohn, Fisher, & Brown, 1961; Hites & Campbell, 1950).

Information bearing directly on the chooser-chosen relationship is contained in one study (Tagirui, Kogan, & Long, 1958) which was directed primarily toward the identification of choosers, as in the studies classed above as type two. Using 106 Ss from a college preparatory boarding school and asking for designations of students with whom they would prefer to room the following year, these investigators found that there was a positive relationship between the status of the chooser and that of the person chosen, significantly different from zero ($p < .05$).

The present study differs from many of these other social perception studies in that it did not ask for judgments of what other people would do. We have concerned ourselves instead with determining the relationships between the choice status of those choosing and those chosen, for positive, negative, and a combination of positive and negative choices.

The Use of Matrices in Obtaining Scores. The second area to which the information contained in the present chapter relates is definitely more technical in nature. The sociometric literature contains a number of theoretical articles recommending the use of matrices in obtaining the basic sociometric score for each individual involved. These recommendations have not been followed by persons making empirical studies.

One of the advantages claimed for the matrix approach is that it retains information about the level of the choosers in evaluating the choices given to an individual. A review of the main papers recommending the use of a matrix approach to choice scores (Festinger, 1949; Forsyth & Katz, 1946; Glanzer & Glaser, 1959; Jamrich, 1960; Katz, 1947, 1953; Luce & Perry, 1949; Proctor & Loomis, 1951) indicates that although this approach was first suggested modestly and tentatively, it later was said by some authors to have displaced the earlier simple procedure of summing choices, although no firm empirical data to support this assertion were presented. The present chapter gives a large-scale illustration of the relations which prevail between the status of choosers and chosen in two large samples of grade school children. The results presented here may not generalize to all other ages; on the other hand, in the absence of any other information about other ages, they may provide a more accurate guide than speculations based upon no data at all.

Information is given below about the correlation between choosers and chosen. It is hoped that these results may provide a factual foundation for theoretical discussions or methods of scoring choice data which has not been available previously to the various proponents of matrix scoring. The results presented here may indicate why there has been such disregard of the matrix scoring approach by empirical workers in this area.

If we use our three peer choice scores, LM, LL, and LM – LL, there are nine possible combinations of scores of choosers and chosen for LM choices alone. These are referred to here and subsequently as "criteria":

1. LM VS. LM   Correlation between LM scores of choosers and LM scores of those they chose as LM.

2. LM VS. LL   Correlation between LM scores of choosers and LL scores of those they chose as LM.

3. LM VS. LM – LL   Correlation between LM scores of choosers and LM – LL scores of those they chose as LM.

4. LL VS. LM   Correlation between LL scores of choosers and LM scores of those they chose as LM.

5. LL VS. LL   Correlation between LL scores of choosers and LL scores of those they chose as LM.

6. LL VS. LM – LL   Correlation between LL scores of choosers and LL scores of those they chose as LM.

7. LM – LL VS. LM   Correlation between LM – LL scores of choosers and LM scores of those they chose as LM.

8. LM – LL VS. LL   Correlation between LM – LL scores of choosers and LL scores of those they chose as LM.

9. LM – LL VS. LM – LL   Correlation between LM – LL scores of choosers and LM – LL scores of those they chose as LM.

There is an exactly corresponding set of pairs of scores of the LL choices; thus there are nine pairs for positive choices and nine pairs for negative choices. The total sample was also broken down for analysis by school grade (3,4,5,6), by socioeconomic status (I,II,III,IV), and by sex (boys, girls, and combined).

The number of separate correlations of each sample can be computed as follows:

There were 9 LM and 9 LL pairs 18
Each of these was computed for boys, for girls, and for boys
and girls combined .... ×3
                                             54
There were 4 school grades, computed separately .... ×4
                                             216
There were 4 socioeconomic levels, computed separately .... ×4
Total set of correlations 864

These correlations could be combined by grades for sex and socio-economic comparisons and by socioeconomic levels for grade comparisons.

The first sample analyzed included approximately 11,000 pupils in grades three through six in one large Minnesota city for which all public schools had been included. In accordance with the strategy of simultaneous replication of the study in the Minnesota and Texas samples, data were available for approximately 19,000 pupils from nineteen cities in Texas. Since it seemed unnecessary to use this entire second sample to get adequate stability in our figures, only 7,312 pupils from Texas were used in obtaining correlations. These consisted of all the pupils for whom data were recorded on two computer tapes; they represented nine cities.

RESULTS

The overall picture for the entire Minnesota and Texas samples is shown in Table 11. If we consider the correlations based on the LM choices for the two samples, it can be seen that none of these 54 correlations between scores of chooser and those whom they chose as LM (boys, girls, total) is negative. They all range between .00 and +.04. The nine categories listed are not uncorrelated, but with a small number of cases these correlations might have been expected to vary much more markedly. If we look at the LL correlations for the two samples, we find that these are consistently negative and range from −.10 to −.20. In terms of accuracy of perception, this means that the LL choices of those who scored higher on LM, LL, or the composite LM − LL were slightly, but only slightly, more in agreement with the group consensus than were the choices of those with lower scores on these three measures. A comparison of samples from the two states shows that they yielded strikingly similar results. Accustomed as we are to working with smaller samples, we would not ordinarily pay any attention to differences between these very small positive correlations of the LM choices. However, for both the LM choices and LL choices it seemed to visual inspection that some of the same correlations were relatively higher in both samples and some were relatively lower. Consequently, rank difference correlations were calculated separately for the nine categories of LM choices and for the nine categories of LL choices. The

Table 11. Chooser-Chosen Correlations for All Grades and Both States

Chooser vs. Chosen	Boys		Girls		Total	
	Minn.[a]	Texas[b]	Minn.[c]	Texas[d]	Minn.[e]	Texas[f]
Like-Most Choices						
LM vs. LM	+.02	+.01	+.02	+.01	+.02	+.01
LM vs. LL	+.02	+.02	+.03	+.02	+.03	+.02
LM vs. LM − LL	+.02	+.01	+.03	+.02	+.02	+.02
LL vs. LM	+.04	+.02	+.04	+.03	+.04	+.03
LL vs. LL	.00	+.01	+.02	+.01	+.01	+.01
LL vs. LM − LL	+.03	+.02	+.03	+.02	+.03	+.02
LM − LL vs. LM	+.03	+.02	+.03	+.02	+.03	+.02
LM − LL vs. LL	.00	+.01	+.02	+.01	+.01	+.01
LM − LL vs. LM − LL	+.02	+.02	+.03	+.02	+.03	+.02
Like-Least Choices						
LM vs. LM	−.15	−.14	−.12	−.15	−.14	−.15
LM vs. LL	−.10	−.10	−.11	−.13	−.11	−.12
LM vs. LM − LL	−.15	−.14	−.13	−.16	−.14	−.15
LL vs. LM	−.14	−.13	−.14	−.16	−.14	−.15
LL vs. LL	−.16	−.15	−.17	−.19	−.16	−.17
LL vs. LM − LL	−.18	−.16	−.18	−.20	−.18	−.18
LM − LL vs. LM	−.18	−.16	−.15	−.18	−.16	−.17
LM − LL vs. LL	−.15	−.14	−.15	−.18	−.16	−.16
LM − LL vs. LM − LL	−.19	−.17	−.18	−.20	−.18	−.19

[a]N = 5,471. [e]N = 5,271.
[d]N = 3,496. [f]N = 7,312.
[b]N = 3,816.
[c]N = 10,742.

rank difference correlation between the sets of positive correlations from the two states for the LM choices was .92, and for the nine pairs of negative correlations for the LL choices was .96.

With very large samples of this kind, it is possible to obtain a degree of stability of values over different samples which is far greater than that ordinarily obtained. These results illustrate sharply the difference between statistical significance and practical importance. The correlations for the nine categories of the LM choices are all positive for the total samples in the two states. This gives a count of eighteen to zero in favor of a positive relationship. On the other hand, the highest correlation in the whole set, from either sample, is .04. The limitations of a correlation of .04 are well known.

When the average correlational values are obtained for boys and girls, no consistent differences appear in the two samples. This is shown in the accompanying tabulation. No difference is consistently in the same direction in the samples from the two states.

	Boys	Girls
Minnesota sample		
LM choices	+.02	+.03
LL choices	−.16	−.15
Texas sample		
LM choices	+.02	+.02
LL choices	−.14	−.17

The combined correlational values for the four grades for positive choices range from +.00 to +.04 in the Minnesota sample and from +.01 to +.03 in the Texas sample. For negative choices the combined correlational values for the four grades for the Minnesota sample are either −.15 or −.16, and the same is true for the Texas sample. Replication in the two widely separated areas gives very similar results and indicates no appreciable shift of values from the third through the sixth grade.

Division into SES levels was available for only the Minnesota sample. The combined correlational values for the positive choices were +.00, +.02, +.02, and +.04, going up the SES scale. Although it is not impossible that this trend might cross-validate, it is too small to be of any importance. For negative choices, the values for the four SES levels, from low to high, were −.16, −.16, −.16, and −.15. Here there is obviously no difference at all.

DISCUSSION

These results throw some light on the two sets of problems mentioned at the beginning of the chapter: social perception, insofar as the present study relates to that somewhat heterogeneous field; and the need for the use of matrices in obtaining sociometric scores.

The present study differs from many of the social perception studies discussed in the early part of this chapter in that no questions were asked requiring a child to estimate what other children would judge him to be like. We have presented information on the relationship between the status of choosing children and of all the children chosen by them, both positively and negatively. The correlations on LM scores between chooser and chosen range between .00 and .04. These are so small as to have neither practical nor theoretical significance. The relationship between chooser and chosen on positive choices alone is lower than in the Tagiuri et al. (1958) study. The correlations between chooser and chosen on LL scores fell, without exception, in the region between −.10 and −.20. These correlations again are too small to be of much interest.

To the extent that the use of matrices for obtaining sociometric scores is based on the supposed need for retaining information concerning *who* chooses as well as how many choose, the lack of relationship between chooser and chosen on positive choices makes the use of matrices in this connection clearly unnecessary. It is, for all practical purposes, also unnecessary for negative choices.

For the Minnesota sample of 10,742, the overall correlation between the positive choice scores of the chooser and chosen was .024. With a sample this size, this is not necessarily a zero correlation. If we had been addicted to elaborate hypothesis formation and to the associated formal hypothesis testing procedures, and if we had hypothesized ahead of time that there would be a positive correlation here, we could assert that the hypothesis was not contradicted by the results. With the same procedure, we got a similar overall correlation of .017 for 7,312 children from Texas. We thus have a neatly cross-validated positive relationship, and if we were to follow a practice which is not uncommon in the behavioral sciences, we would say with considerable fanfare that the number of choices a child receives is a function of the choice status of those who vote for him.

Actually, of course, from any practical point of view, these correlations are zeros. Thus, the concern of the matrix advocates who assert that it is necessary to retain information concerning the status of choosers is seen to be unfounded.

It is quite conceivable that there may exist samples which differ enough from these that the present results will not apply. However, rational considerations indicate that the present results may be generalizable to many markedly different samples. In the case of those receiving many positive votes (the "stars") it would obviously be necessary for them to draw votes from individuals at all score levels. Similarly, in the case of those receiving no positive choices, the choice status of the non-choosers would obviously not matter. Owing to practical difficulties associated with negative nominations, the large majority of studies deal only with positive choices.

The situation with respect to LL choices is slightly different. For the Minnesota sample of 10,742, the overall correlation between chooser and chosen was −.152. On cross-validation in Texas, the overall correlation on a sample of 7,312 was −.160. This means that youngsters of higher choice status were *very slightly* more accurate with their LL votes (in terms of group consensus) than low status children. Although these correlations are firm and differ little, they are still not large enough to make much practical difference. It would be definitely misleading with correlations of this size to make an unqualified statement that "Like Least votes of children of higher sociometric status are more similar to group consensus than those of low status children." It is possible to find statements of this type which are based on relations no stronger than this one, and on much smaller samples, being detached from their contexts and pursuing independent existences of their own in many behavioral science areas.

Within the total samples, separate breakdowns were made for sex and school grade. None of these variables made enough difference to have any practical significance.

TWIN AND SIBLING RESEMBLANCES*

Many variables contribute to the development of personality characteristics. Among this large set, one important subset is the family in

*Part of this section was published in S. B. Sells and M. Roff, "Family Influ-

which children have been born and reared. A general consideration of this problem has been presented by Roff (1950), who compared the family resemblance correlations of a wide variety of personality characteristics as they were presented in the research literature up to that time. No comparable research results concerning the resemblance of twins and siblings on peer acceptance-rejection have been found. It was possible in this study to get resemblance correlations on groups which are large enough for the results to have substantial stability. This chapter presents findings on twin and sibling resemblances, and on further subdivisions of siblings according to sex and number of siblings, contained in the four school grades of this study.

These twin and sibling resemblance coefficients do not, of course, indicate the relative contribution of heredity and environment. Since most of these children were brought up by their own parents, we cannot separate the effects of biological inheritance from those of the environmental family situation in which the children grew up.

The most sensible procedure to follow seemed to be to investigate various possible breakdowns into subsets of both the twin and sibling groups. In the case of intelligence, the differences between family correlations for males and females are not striking. The correlations between sisters and between brothers are not markedly different from those between brothers and sisters. On the other hand, it is possible to find personality characteristics where the sex of the subjects must be taken into consideration, and it seemed obviously desirable to break down both twin and sibling samples on the basis of sex. Although it is possible that there may be either more or less resemblance in peer status among brothers than among sisters, no theoretical formulations which would lead to such expectations were found. On the other hand, since certain personality characteristics do sometimes function differently for girls than for boys, it might be expected that the sibling resemblance among sets of brothers and among sets of sisters would be at least slightly higher than that between siblings opposite in sex.

Twins constitute a special group among siblings. They are divisible into fraternal twins, who are considered no more alike genetically

ence as Reflected in Peer Acceptance-Rejection and Resemblance of Siblings as Compared with Random Sets of School Children," *Psychology in the Schools*, 1965, 2, 133–137. Excerpts, in slightly different form, are included here by permission of the publisher.

than ordinary brothers and sisters, and identical or monozygotic twins, who are considered to have the same genetic makeup. It is possible to attempt to appraise the relative influence of genetic makeup and environmental factors through statistical analyses of correlations between fraternal twins on the one hand and identical twins on the other. Loehlin (1965) has done some interesting work along this line. Whether or not such studies would give the same results as studies in which there has been actual separation of children from their true parents early in life is not certain. Obviously experimentation is impossible here. In any case, this seems to be the first extensive data on twin and sibling resemblance in peer status.

Sample. The subjects of the present investigation are children from the entire first year Minnesota sample ($N = 17,075$) and from eleven of the nineteen Texas cities which participated in the study ($N = 10,405$). With the aid of school personnel and records, the sets of siblings in these two groups were identified. Since the first-year sample included third- through sixth-graders, pairs of siblings are much more common than larger numbers of siblings — those siblings who were below third grade or over sixth would not be included. There were 4,273 sets of two siblings and 650 sets of three siblings in the total sample of 27,480 in the four-grade range.

In addition to the correlations among siblings, similar correlations were computed for a sample of unrelated pairs of children, randomly drawn. It was found, as indicated in Figure 2, that these correlations between unrelated individuals did not differ significantly from zero and hence are negligible.

The twins were located by identifying siblings with the same birth dates. If a sample is small, it is possible to make elaborate biological tests to distinguish between identical and fraternal twins. However, it has been shown that identical twins can be located almost as well by simply asking a set of adult identical twins if they consider themselves identical (Jablon et al., 1967). Therefore, in view of our sample size, it was decided to ask school personnel who knew the children whether or not they regarded each set of twins as identical or fraternal. Of course, if the identification of twins as identical or fraternal was poor, this would be reflected in the correlations. Since the investigators were physically closer to the schools in Minnesota than in Texas, it was pos-

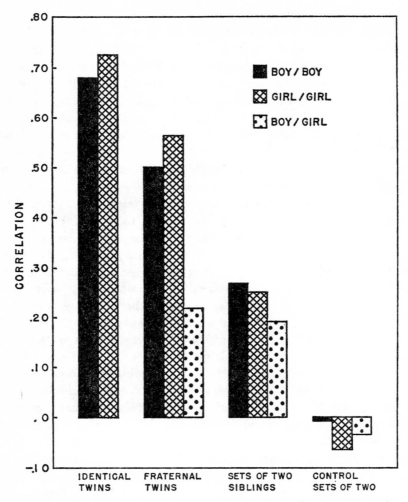

Figure 2. Intraclass correlations of Like Most minus Like Least scores for twins, sets of two siblings, and control sets of two. Number of pairs: identical twins — 33 boy/boy, 41 girl/girl; fraternal twins — 47 boy/boy, 31 girl/girl, 85 boy/girl; siblings — 1,114 boy/boy, 1,026 girl/girl, 2,133 boy/girl; controls — 1,244 boy/boy, 1,148 girl/girl, 1,849 boy/girl.

sible for them to have closer contact with the school personnel and to obtain multiple judgments from teachers and school nurses. Hence, the distinction between identical and fraternal twins was somewhat more accurate in the Minnesota than in the Texas sample.

Results. The overall results are shown graphically in Figure 2, using only the pairs for non-twin siblings. The LM – LL correlations for all the sets of siblings, fraternal twins, and identical twins are shown in Table 12. The sibling correlations for sets of two (non-twins) and

Table 12. Intraclass Correlations for Various Sets of Siblings on LM – LL

Sets	Same Sex			Unlike Sex		
	Boys	Girls	Both[a]	Boy/Girl	Boy/Boy/Girl	Boy/Girl/Girl
Identical twins						
N	33	41	74			
Correlation	.68	.72	.70			
Fraternal twins						
N	47	31	78	85		
Correlation	.50	.56	.52	.27		
Non-twin sets of two						
N	1,114	1,026	2,140	2,133		
Correlation	.32	.30	.31	.24		
Sets of three						
N	89	97			233	231
Correlation	.24	.31			.32	.31

[a]Combined same-sex sibling pairs.

three are essentially the same size, except that the boy/girl correlation for the sets of two and the boy/boy/boy correlation in the sets of three are slightly lower than the others. No explanation for these two differences is apparent. The most interesting correlations are those for identical and fraternal twins and non-twin sibling pairs, which show an ordered change downward with each successive group shown.

The question arose whether the peer scores and Teacher Ratings for identical twins would be affected by their being in the same or different classes. The resemblance coefficients for both peer choices and Teacher Ratings were somewhat higher for 35 pairs of identical twins in the same class than for 36 pairs in different classes. However, this difference did not hold up consistently for fraternal like-sex twins and fraternal unlike-sex twins, so that this result must be regarded as only suggestive.

Other Scores with Breakdowns. The correlational values for five sets of scores — LM, LL, LM – LL, TR, and combined peer-teacher score — are given in Appendix Tables 3–5. Appendix Table 3 presents correlations for these five scores for non-twin sibling sets of two and three in all possible combinations (boy/boy, etc.). Appendix Table 4 breaks these scores down by identical and fraternal twins and non-twin siblings of like or unlike sex. Appendix Table 5 is similar except that male and female pairs are compared, and results are separated by state. Comparison of the different scores shows that the combined peer-teacher score rises to .77 for identical twins and correspondingly for the others.

Little in the way of consistent sex differences was found between male and female pairs on the various peer scores. The unlike-sex fraternal twins and non-twin siblings show less resemblance than the like-sex pairs. Comparison of correlations between identical twins, fraternal twins, and non-twin siblings by state indicated that for the identical twins the resemblance coefficients are somewhat higher in Minnesota than in Texas. This is thought to be attributable to greater accuracy of twin identification in Minnesota. For the fraternal twins, there are no consistent differences between the two states. For the non-twin siblings, the resemblance coefficients for Texas are slightly larger than those for Minnesota. On the whole, the differences between the results from the two states are not striking.

Taken all together, the correlations presented here give a clear and consistent picture of different degrees of family resemblance. On the other hand, the relatively low size of the correlations among ordinary siblings emphasizes the fact that the outcomes for people growing up within the same family can vary widely. Still, the degree of relationship shown is large enough to indicate the desirability of obtaining information about the families in order to relate this to the peer status of children. Information about the relations between family variables and child social adjustment are presented below in Chapters 6 and 7.

INTELLIGENCE, SOCIOECONOMIC LEVEL, AND CHOICE STATUS

It has long been known that there is a moderate correlation between intelligence and choice status and between intelligence and socioeconomic level. The multivariate analysis reported in the present chapter compares the intelligence of high- and low-choice children by sex, socioeconomic level, and choice status.

Almack's (1922) is the earliest study combining intelligence and choice status. His aim was somewhat different from ours, but his procedure was sufficiently similar to later procedures to make it worth describing: "To get at some evaluation of the influence of intelligence in determining the choice of associates among children, the following study was made. The subjects were 387 children in grades 4 to 7 inclusive, of the public schools of San Jose, California. The National Intelligence Test was first given, and mental ages and IQ's computed. The pupils were next directed (1) to write the name of the boy or girl in his school whom he would select to help him if he were given some work to do, for which the person selected was well fitted; and (2) to write the name of the boy and the name of the girl in their school whom they would first invite to a party, assuming they were each given one" (p. 529). Almack reported positive correlations between the IQ's of the choosing children and the children they chose.

Hardy (1937) made the earliest study comparing IQ and choice status directly, for a grade school sample obtained from schools in Joliet, Illinois. Choices of desired associates were obtained during an interview, and intelligence was appraised by the Stanford-Binet. A correlation of .37 was reported between number of choices received and IQ. Later studies essentially similar to this one commonly obtained correlational values of this general magnitude (Bonney, 1942, 1943 a&b, 1944, 1946; Davis, 1957; Gallagher & Crowder, 1956; Johnson, 1950; McGahan, 1940). On the other hand, Jennings (1943) in a study of adolescent girls in a training school found a correlation of only .04 between IQ and choices received. This result is not typical of those obtained with unselected public school samples.

Two studies have gone beyond this gross correlational approach. Grossmann and Wrighter (1948), employing a sample of four sixth-grade classes in a university community, compared the relationships between intelligence and sociometric status using a three-interval breakdown of intelligence levels. They concluded that "intelligence did make a difference up to a certain point — normal intelligence — but beyond that it did not materially affect the selection-rejection score" (p. 354). This study is somewhat unsatisfactory since the middle intelligence group was defined so broadly as to leave few cases for the upper and lower groups. However, it is of interest since an hypothesis of a differential relation between intelligence level and sociometric status is stated.

The second of these studies, by Porterfield and Schlichting (1961), compared reading achievement scores obtained using Test I, Paragraph Meaning, of the Stanford Achievement Test with various pupil characteristics, including sociometric scores. Their sample, drawn from sixth-grade pupils in the Tulsa Public Schools, had a total of 981 pupils drawn about equally from schools of high, middle, and low SES. As would be expected from the studies of intelligence, they found a firm relationship between this achievement test and sociometric status. When results by socioeconomic levels were examined, Porterfield and Schlichting found a relationship between achievement scores and social acceptability status in the high and middle group, but the relation between test scores and social acceptability was not significant in the low SES schools, although it was in the expected direction. This is similar to the Grossmann and Wrighter study in suggesting that the relationship between an intellectual variable and sociometric status is different at various socioeconomic levels, but data are opposing in the reported level at which the difference occurred. It is possible to hypothesize in either of these directions or in still other ways. In the absence of clearer support from the literature than is afforded by the studies reviewed here, we simply analyzed the material to see what we would find. There was no compelling reason to hypothesize that a difference would occur at any point in the scale, or that no difference would appear at any level.

The sample used here included 2,800 fourth-grade children of both sexes from all the public schools in one Minnesota city. The fourth grade in this city was employed because these children had been given the Lorge-Thorndike Intelligence Test during the school year, and because this city was the largest for which results were available for the entire city.

The schools were classified into four approximately equal groups (quartiles) on the basis of the income and educational levels of the census tracts comprising their districts, as described on page 18.

At each of our four SES levels, the group of high girls and high boys was defined as consisting of all those with standard scores 1 SD or more above the mean on LM – LL. A corresponding group of low girls and low boys was defined as consisting of those with a LM − LL score 1 SD below the mean. When the mean IQ for each of these groups was computed, the values shown in Table 13 and Figure 3 were obtained (mean IQ values for all fourth-graders by SES are also presented in Table 13).

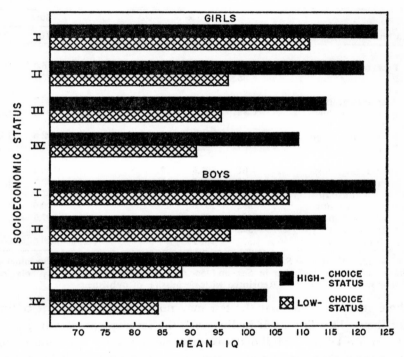

Figure 3. The IQ and choice status of girls and boys in relation to socio-economic background. Reprinted with permission of the publisher from M. Roff and S. B. Sells, "Relations between Intelligence and Sociometric Status in Groups Differing in Sex and Socioeconomic Background," *Psychological Reports*, 1965, 16, 511–516.

There was a consistent sex difference of about 5 IQ points in favor of the girls at all four socioeconomic levels and for the total groups. This did not affect the general pattern of differences between high- and low-choice groups at the different socioeconomic levels. Inspection of Figure 3 shows that at all four levels the differences between the high and low groups for both sexes are about the same.

There is a difference of about 15 to 20 IQ points between the high-

and low-choice groups at various socioeconomic levels. The only exception to this is in the top level, where the differences for girls and boys are only 11.5 and 14.3 points, respectively. The smaller SD's of

Table 13. Lorge-Thorndike IQ (Verbal) and Sociometric Status by Sex and SES, Fourth Grade

	Girls			Boys		
SES and Rating	N	M_{IQ}	SD	N	M_{IQ}	SD
SES I						
Peer rating, high	53	118.8	10.9	64	118.0	10.1
Peer rating, low	53	107.3	14.9	55	103.7	17.6
SES II						
Peer rating, high	53	115.9	12.4	65	109.7	13.5
Peer rating, low	46	93.8	14.5	49	94.3	13.5
SES III						
Peer rating, high	49	109.7	11.6	53	102.6	16.4
Peer rating, low	54	92.6	12.7	54	86.1	14.8
SES IV						
Peer rating, high	61	105.5	13.3	57	100.4	15.0
Peer rating, low	50	88.7	15.0	46	82.5	13.3
SES I: Total group	332	113.2		342	108.9	
SES II: Total group	332	107.0		376	99.5	
SES III: Total group	399	102.2		398	97.5	
SES IV: Total group	312	96.4		309	92.0	
Grand Total	1,375	104.7		1,425	99.6	

SOURCE: M. Roff & S. B. Sells, "Relations between Intelligence and Sociometric Status in Groups Differing in Sex and Socioeconomic Background," *Psychological Reports*, 1965, 16, 511–516. Reprinted with permission of publisher.

these groups suggest that the test may not have had sufficient ceiling for them. This finding is in line with the impressions obtained from earlier work with childhood case histories — namely, an intelligence level above the average of the peer group is an asset in a wide variety of groups. A child of either sex with an IQ of 80 in a low socioeconomic group or a child with an IQ of 100 in an upper socioeconomic group is at a real social disadvantage.

In statistical terms, these findings can be said to indicate that there would be no marked departure from linearity if correlation coefficients based on the entire sample were computed. Table 13 does not itself yield correlational values, because the middle group has been omitted. Figure 3 indicates that the difference in IQ between the high and low boys and girls is essentially the same in all socioeconomic quartiles.

PEER STATUS IN RELATION TO BIRTH ORDER

The problem of the effect of birth order among siblings has received attention from psychologists and others interested in human behavior for at least a hundred years. Two of the earliest studies are those by Mitchell (1866), who studied the relative frequency of mental retardation among firstborn children, and the classic study by Galton (1874), who studied birth order among English men of science. Since that time there have been a large number of studies, which have shifted somewhat in emphasis from one period to another. A review of this literature up to 1932 was prepared by Harold Jones (1933) for the *Handbook of Child Psychology*, with a thoroughness and a concern for methodological problems which is rarely found today. For example, he reported correlations of –.27 and –.33 for family size with social status and IQ, respectively. Thus, children from large families would reflect both a lower SES and a lower intelligence level, for whatever significance that would have for any characteristic being studied. It seemed clear to him that "Psychological differences within the various birth orders have, as a rule, been small in magnitude, and they have not always been in the same direction in different samples." A second intensive survey of the influence of birth order was presented by Murphy, Murphy, and Newcomb (1937), who tabulated a large number of studies involving delinquency, intelligence, behavior problems, personality traits, school performance, sensitivity to pain, dominance feeling, fame, nervousness, jealousy, aggressiveness, stuttering, emotionality, neuroticism, atheism, political attitudes, and happiness. They observed that, "psychological position in the family is of the utmost importance for the development of social behavior, but 'psychological position' is by no means completely dependent on birth order." Their tabulation of research studies "gives a digest of the results of a number of birth-order studies which tend to be inconclusive or contradictory." Since the samples included varied widely in age, educational level, characteristic studied, and so on, it is not surprising that the results presented did not give a coherent picture. There have been many studies in the more than thirty years since the Murphy, Murphy, and Newcomb review was written, but the situation now is not greatly different from that described by them. No single set of well-established findings has received general acceptance.

Since we had peer status measures on a large sample, and since information about birth order could be obtained at a relatively low cost, a pilot study (Sells & Roff, 1964a), followed by a more comprehensive study, of the relation between birth order and peer status was carried out in several Texas cities. The results are clear, but the differences are small enough that it seemed unnecessary to replicate this on the Minnesota sample. This is almost the only study of this general type that was not replicated in both states.

In the pilot study, birth order data were obtained for 1,013 pupils constituting the complete samples for two Texas school districts for whom first-year scores were available. For the main study, birth order data were obtained for 2,957 pupils in two additional school districts for whom both first- and second-year scores were available. The averaging of scores for the first two years gave a somewhat more reliable score than that of a single year.

The birth order of the sample was coded according to six categories: only child, oldest child, second child of two, second child of more than two, middle child of four or more, and youngest child.

The mean values for each of the scores for the six birth order positions are shown in Table 14. Inspection of this table indicates, first, that the rank of the different categories is approximately the same for the different scores (LM, TR). Whatever differences occurred are quite

Table 14. Comparison of Peer Scores and Birth Order in Texas Sample $(N = 2,957)$ Using Combined First- and Second-Year Scores

Birth Order	N	LM	LL	LM−LL	TR	2(LM−LL)+TR
Second of two	444	5.18	5.10	5.16	5.11	5.15
Youngest	390	5.12	5.05	5.11	5.07	5.10
Oldest	839	5.05	5.01	5.04	5.07	5.05
Second of more than two..	536	5.04	5.01	5.02	5.04	5.03
Only	312	5.04	5.03	5.04	5.00	5.02
Middle of four or more ...	436	4.90	4.91	4.90	4.91	4.87

consistent over scores. The mean values for all scores of all categories except "middle of four or more" are slightly above 5.0. The fact that only those with scores obtained in both years were used resulted in mean scores slightly higher than those for the first year sample alone. Those lost from moving away had scores slightly below the average of those who stayed.

The middle-of-four-or-more category is noticeably lower than any other. This result would be due not only to any possible adverse effects of large family size as such, but also to any adverse effects of below-average IQ and SES of the family, both of which are related to peer status scores. Whether or not family size would remain a significantly adverse factor if only those equal in SES to two-child families were included is not known. For the other five categories, the difference between means of each pair of adjacent categories is very small — for example, that between the oldest and the youngest child is only .05. In the pilot study the combined peer-teacher score shown in Table 14 also had a value of 4.87. The other scores, based only on the first-year scores and obtained from a smaller sample, differed somewhat in rank from those shown in Table 14: the youngest child and the only child were the highest in the pilot study, whereas the oldest child was fifth instead of third from the top. These differences are too small to be of any consequence, and the safest conclusion seems to be that there is little difference owing to birth order between peer status scores among all the categories except the middle of four or more.

5

Children with
Spanish Surnames

The problem of the effect of differences in racial or ethnic background and peer acceptance-rejection is still of major interest many years after the first such study was made. In reviewing earlier work, Gronlund (1959) observes that, "Where racial cleavages exist in a community, these cleavages are reflected in children's sociometric choices. However, where racial integration has been in effect for some time, children's sociometric choices freely cross race lines. Older studies, by Moreno (1934) and Criswell (1939), have shown distinct cleavages between white and Negro children, with the members of both groups most frequently choosing companions from among their own racial group. Both studies were conducted in a large metropolitan area where segregation was common. More recent studies have shown that where racial integration has been in effect for a period of years, racial cleavages are not as apparent in sociometric results" (p. 218). With the exception of black children in segregated schools in Texas, racial identifications were not available for our samples in the school records. In Minnesota, when the question arose in public discussion as to the concentration of blacks which existed in certain schools, this information was not available and had to be obtained by the school authorities by making a head count, in which each school was asked to report the number of its black students.

It was possible, however, to identify those individuals with Spanish surnames, as was done in the 1960 census for five southwestern states (Arizona, California, Colorado, New Mexico, and Texas), and to

94

compare this group with the total remaining sample, predominantly white, in both states. An intensive search of the literature has turned up few comparisons of peer status of those with Spanish surnames and others. Loomis (1943) compared peer scores of the two groups in two New Mexico high schools. In one of these the proportion of "Anglo's" was slightly less than one-fourth; in the other almost two-thirds of the sample were Anglo. These high school students were not asked who they liked most or liked least, but were instructed to "write in names of boys or girls you pal or play with most at school" (p. 16). In other words, an attempt was made to have actual associations reported rather than preferences. It was found that a larger number in each group associated more with members of their own groups than would have occurred by chance distribution. Although his sample included only thirty students in third and fourth grades, the possibility was indicated that ethnically based cleavage might be less at the grade school than at the high school level.

Both common sense and the literature suggest the necessity for caution in generalizing from studies of ethnic status at one particular place and time to a different place and time. The results to be presented here were obtained in 1961 and 1962 in Minnesota and Texas. Texas is, of course, adjacent to Mexico, and the Spanish-American city of San Antonio, for example, was substantial in size long before the splitting off of Texas from Mexico. Minnesota is far from Mexico, but there are nevertheless enough persons with Spanish surnames, primarily of Mexican background, to permit a meaningful study and comparison with the results obtained in Texas.

The control groups were obtained by taking an adjacent non-Spanish surname from the same class roster as each Spanish surname. An exception to this was the small number of schools which consisted largely of children with Spanish surnames. In these cases, additional controls were obtained from neighboring schools of similar socio-economic status.

The results obtained by a comparison of Spanish and non-Spanish surname children in the two states are presented in Table 15, for the entire sample of boys and girls, grades three through six combined, for the two states. For the LM scores for the total Texas sample, there is a slight but definite difference in average between the Spanish surname and control groups. This difference does not appear in the total Minnesota sample. For the LL scores, there is no significant difference between the Spanish surname groups and their controls in the two states. The LM – LL score simply reflects its two component scores. The TR's also show a slight difference in favor of the controls in Texas but show no difference at all in Minnesota.

Broken down by sex, the Spanish surname pupils' LM scores are slightly lower than the controls in Texas, but not in Minnesota. LL score differences are negligible, and LM – LL score again reflects its component scores. The TR's show practically no difference between Spanish surname boys and controls in each state but show a small, significant difference in favor of the controls for the girls in Texas. In general, although there is some indication of a greater difference between the two groups for girls than for boys, it is too small to be of practical significance.

For the Minnesota sample only, a comparison of scores of Spanish surname and control pupils at each of the four grade levels was made in order to see whether there was a significant shift from one grade to another. There is no indication of any trend toward either more or less difference between the two groups from the third to the sixth grade.

Other points of interest were whether or not there would be

Table 15. Comparison of Mean Peer and Teacher Rating Scores for Children with Spanish and Non-Spanish Surnames

Score and Group	Boys		Girls		Total	
	Texas[a]	Minn.[b]	Texas[c]	Minn.[d]	Texas[e]	Minn.[f]
LM						
Spanish surname	4.9*	5.2	4.6*	5.0	4.7*	5.1
Control	5.2	5.0	5.1	5.1	5.2	5.0
LL						
Spanish surname	5.0	5.1	4.8	4.9	4.9	5.0
Control	5.1	4.9	5.0	5.1	5.0	5.0
LM – LL						
Spanish surname	4.9	5.1	4.7*	4.9	4.8*	5.1
Control	5.1	5.0	5.0	5.1	5.1	5.0
TR						
Spanish surname	4.9	4.9	4.7*	4.9	4.8*	5.0
Control	5.0	5.0	5.2	5.1	5.1	5.0

[a]$N = 311$ in each group.　　　[b]$N = 191$ in each group.
[c]$N = 329$ in each group.　　　[d]$N = 198$ in each group.
[e]$N = 640$ in each group.　　　[f]$N = 389$ in each group.
*$p < .01$ for differences between Spanish-surname and control children.

marked differences between the Spanish surname group and the control group if the Minnesota sample were broken down by SES and by the proportion of Spanish-American children in a school. Results of these comparisons are shown in Table 16. SES groups I, II, and IV-b are

Table 16. Comparison of Mean Peer and Teacher Rating Scores for Children with Spanish and Non-Spanish Surnames, Minnesota Only

Score and Group	SES I (N = 15)	SES II (N = 25)	SES III (N = 89)	SES IV-a[a] (N = 108)	SES IV-b[b] (N = 152)
LM					
Spanish surname	5.2	4.9	5.1	5.2	5.0
Control	4.8	4.9	5.1	5.1	4.9
LL					
Spanish surname	5.5	4.9	5.0	5.0	5.1
Control	5.1	4.9	5.1	4.9	4.9
LM – LL					
Spanish surname	5.1	4.9	5.1	5.1	5.1
Control	5.0	4.9	5.1	5.0	4.9
TR					
Spanish surname	5.2	4.8	5.0	5.0	5.0
Control	5.0	5.0	5.0	5.0	5.0

[a]This group contains fifteen schools in quartile IV with low percentages of Spanish-surname children.
[b]This group contains the two schools in quartile IV with high percentages of Spanish-surname children (a smaller school with 61 per cent Spanish-surname children and a larger school with 26 per cent Spanish-surname children).

from one Minnesota city only, since only that city had schools with 26 per cent or more of the pupils with Spanish surnames. SES III and IV-a groups include the second Minnesota city, all schools of which had low percentages of Spanish surname children.

The Spanish surname pupils were found most frequently in the SES IV schools, but the numbers shown in the table exaggerate this effect since the SES I and II pupils were from one city only. However, if we combine the IV-a and IV-b numbers shown in the table it can be seen that there are almost three times as many Spanish surname pupils in group IV as in group III.

The comparisons across SES show no consistent trend whatever. At all SES levels and in group IV schools with a low percentage of Spanish surname children as well as in its two schools with a higher percentage of Spanish surname pupils, there are simply no apparent trends of any kind in relation to SES or to proportion of pupils with Spanish surnames in the schools.

The nineteen Texas cities were classified on the basis of location in or out of a metropolitan area. This enabled a comparison between large communities (in) and small communities (out). No significant mean differences on any of the peer scores were found between Spanish-American children in large and small communities.

Although occasional differences between groups of one kind or another have been discussed thus far, these differences have in no case been large enough to be of much practical consequence. But with a large sample, it is possible to get technically significant differences between two groups when the actual differences are very small. To illustrate more clearly the practical significance of some of the differences found, point biserial correlation coefficients (McNemar, 1962) are shown in the accompanying tabulation for the Spanish surname groups and their controls. It can be seen that the highest of these is .16 for Texas girls. These correlations are not large enough to indicate any substantial degree of relationship. Hence, the effect of Spanish surnames (and all their correlates) on peer status is small in both states.

	LM – LL
Texas boys	–.105
Texas girls	–.158
Minnesota boys	+.050
Minnesota girls	–.105

To give concrete illustrations of specific cases included in the statistics presented above, condensed qualitative descriptions of certain children are presented below. In general, the high-choice Spanish surname pupils sound very much like other high-choice pupils, and the low-choice pupils, whether in a classroom situation in which they are the only member of their ethnic group or in a school in which their ethnic group is in the majority, tend to show personal characteristics or personality problems similar to those of low-choice children generally. The first child described is a high-choice boy from a school above average SES, in which the number of pupils with his ethnic background is very small.

❧❧❧❧❧

Dennis (fifth grade) is a healthy, dark-complexioned, dark-haired Mexican boy with a medium build. He is probably the most popular boy in the room and has frequently been chosen president.

He is a very lighthearted, carefree young man who is nice to everyone and is well liked by his peers. He has a sister in class, and the other youngsters who like the sister also like him. His ability is about average. He has some difficulty doing his academic work. He sometimes acts like he is a big shot, and is somewhat of an egotist. Discipline, when administered, is accepted with some resentment. However, he is generally well mannered, conscientious, and quite accepting of responsibility. In the classroom he is in the low reading group, and seems to lack motivation. He is interested in working with his hands and shows some interest and creative ability in art. On the playground this boy participates freely and is a good sport. He is usually selected captain. His classmates admire and accept him, and he enjoys his popularity. Dennis' mother has been to school for conferences. She is a calm, sweet, very understanding woman. This boy comes from a close-knit family. He seems very proud of being Mexican, which is not a problem in this vicinity.

<hr/>

The second case, also from a school above average SES, is a least-liked child. Her difficulty seems more associated with her scholastic problems than with any particular prejudice. As indicated on page 89, there is a substantial relationship between intelligence and choice status at all socioeconomic levels.

Pilar (fifth grade) is very clean and neatly dressed. She is different from the rest of the children in her class because she is quiet, very shy, and somewhat withdrawn. However, this may be part of her culture group as she's a member of a minority in this class. She has no particular strengths or weaknesses; however, scholastically she is somewhat slow and schoolwork is extremely difficult for her. On the playground she participates quite well in all activities. In the classroom she does her best in all her work, and is never out of order. She has a few friends among the other students; however, she is very reserved. She gets along quite well with the teacher, is very cooperative, kind, and helpful.

She seems to be more withdrawn and quiet since the Christmas holiday. Classmates seem hardly to notice her, probably because she is very shy and does not want to participate.

Her mother seemed cooperative and understands the child is having difficulty in school. All involved feel this child's difficulty in school is due to her inability to compete scholastically with the rest of her class.

≈≈≈≈≈

A third case is that of a high-choice boy from a school of lower-middle SES. There is a suggestion here of friction associated with movement into the neighborhood of others of his ethnic group, but his peer choice scores obtained toward the end of the school year remained high.

Until recently Tony (sixth grade) was the only Mexican boy in the room. There had been very few in the whole school until this past year. He is outstanding in appearance and also in noisy aggressiveness. He's a good-looking boy with a fairly large head and an enormous mouth.

His strengths are that he is loyal, energetic, industrious at times; but then again he has weaknesses in that he follows the wrong crowd in the room. He's unable to make wise decisions in choosing companions. He is more advanced than most his age in picking up remarks and making inferences of a suggestive nature, particularly on the playground.

On the playground he works very hard. He has a short, squatty body that doesn't adapt too well to physical activity but he's a good team member. In the classroom he works very hard if pressure is kept on him. He's not quite up to the grade, needs more help than most children, and is easily distracted.

In relation to other students, he's gregarious, sensitive, and would be deeply hurt if he felt that he was not liked. He likes people. Tony could be a charmer. He's flirtatious, has kind of a twinkly expression and is somewhat of an apple polisher; but he considers his peers' values and sometimes can be unmannerly if he feels that this type of behavior would be more acceptable to the rather rough crowd of boys that he associates with.

His classmates find him amusing and he plays up to them. He is not mean. The teacher feels that he would be chosen by some as being liked for being amusing and loyal, but that he is disliked by others. As other families of Mexican background moved into the community after being displaced in another part of the city, the tension in the community and the school grew and seemed to build up around Tony although he has been in this school several years. The teacher had him in second grade some years earlier and thought him very cute. He was very well accepted at that time. The teacher feels that Tony is realistic and has his feet on the ground. For instance, he has remarked that he'll have to go to work when he's through high school.

Tony's mother seems to be too old to have a child this young. The teacher wondered if she might not really be his grandmother. There are several older children in the family who are married. There is no father figure. Mother has long been widowed and is receiving welfare. Mother has attended conferences and PTA, where she brought an interpreter as she does not understand English.

✧✧✧✧✧

The next case is a girl of average-choice status from a lower–middle-class school. Her qualitative description sounds ordinary in every way, and there is no indication or suggestion that her ethnic background is particularly related to her peer status.

Andrea (fifth grade) is pleasant looking, clean, well dressed, rather average in looks. She is one of the few children in the room of Mexican background. A good worker, she tries hard but doesn't excel except in physical education. She's rather athletic for a girl. She's not really outstanding in any area but she cooperates well. She has some weaknesses in arithmetic, but she catches up.

Her behavior on the playground is very good. She plays hard and well. She has good motor control. In the classroom her behavior is excellent. She has caused not a minute of trouble. In relation to other children her behavior is very good. She's thoughtful of others and doesn't push herself forward. In relation to the teacher, she's very obedient. She does her assignments, is a good writer and is good in spelling. She made normal progress during the year.

Her classmates like her. They would just as soon have her on their team as any other child. She's treated like any other average child in the room because she is good natured, happy, responds well, isn't boisterous or loud, cooperates, and is considerate. When it is her turn, she does what is supposed to be done, but she won't knock anyone down to get the ball or get her chance. In class she volunteers.

The teacher knows nothing of her family background. Neither parent has come to school.

✧✧✧✧✧

The next boy had high peer scores in a school in the lowest quartile socioeconomically. He is one of those for whom qualitative descriptions were obtained again in the sixth grade, so descriptions of him from different teachers at two different times are presented here.

Roger (in third grade) is of Mexican or Spanish descent, has very dark skin and a characteristic sad expression. He has a very good build and is very agile. In other physical respects he is an average third-grader.

He excels in athletics because he is stronger than most of the other children and very well coordinated. He is a good student and very dependable. However, he is too talkative at times and also somewhat aggressive with other children from time to time.

The teacher feels that his aggressiveness is in essence a strong bid for leadership and he tends to lord it over the other children, especially in outdoor play. Often in the classroom he gives directions to the other students. On the playground Roger enters into the spirit of things and plays very well. The other children like to have him on their team. In the classroom he talks out loud a lot. For instance, when an assignment is given he hollers out, "What page?" The teacher has a difficult time keeping him down; he likes to get out of his seat and go about the room.

In relationships with others he is somewhat aggressive. Roger respects the teacher and she merely has to remind him to calm down. Those who do not like him complain that he is not fair, that he punches them, trips them, or takes things away from them.

Roger receives good care from home and apparently has an average situation there.

〜〜〜〜〜

Roger (in sixth grade) is a short, slender, dark-eyed youngster. He is very neat and clean in his appearance and usually has a well-scrubbed look. He is very well coordinated and takes pride in his athletic ability. When he is out of order in the classroom or on the playground, he responds with a very blank, stupid look. He is very boisterous in his teasing and chiding other children when they make mistakes. He is above average in intelligence, but is an under-achiever. He is in school because he has to be, but shows no real interest in it. He is constantly testing the authority of the teacher and of any other adults in the building. He pushes, shoves, and forces the teacher sometimes to lose patience.

His behavior on the playground is usually good although he has to be the number one person in any competition. He has a group of followers. He cannot accept decisions that are given by an umpire or a person in authority. In a committee assignment, he usually follows the rules unless he is placed with one or two youngsters he considers superior to him in athletic ability. He has to be directed a great deal of the time or he is busy socializing with everyone around him. He wants to be a boxer and the teacher feels he has the ability to carry it through.

He resents the teacher's authority and he mutters under his breath in a rather belittling manner, "yes sir" or "no sir." The teacher feels that Roger has little respect for him. The teacher likes Roger and Roger is very aware of this. He can now recognize that other people do have rights and has, upon occasion, even interceded for an underdog.

The mother constantly calls him "my little Roggie," which he obviously now resents. The mother is active in the community — she is on the PTA board; but the relation of the parents to the community seems rather poor. They seem to be considered somewhat as troublemakers by their neighbors.

∞∞∞∞∞

This girl had high peer scores in a school in the lowest quartile socioeconomically in which only a small percentage of other students were of similar ethnic background. She shows many of the characteristics of popular girls from any of the schools in the study.

Connie (sixth grade) is a very attractive, twelve-year-old Mexican girl. She is more mature physically than most of her girl friends. She is well adjusted, well cared for, well mannered, very polite, and has a most pleasing voice. She is set off from other girls because of her pretty clothes. She comes from a very fine family as far as cooperation is concerned. Both parents come to PTA and are very interested in the children's school achievement. There is a good relationship between members of the family.

She has been president of the student council this year, is very popular with everyone, and has the ability to get along. Her only apparent weakness seems to be that she is not quite as bright as the others in the room. She is an overachiever, although academically she's a little low and she has to work hard to keep up with the group. She has good work habits and drives to finish things and do her best.

In the classroom she is pleasant and cheerful, polite to the teachers, helpful in the room, and is very well liked by all. She does many nice things for others. She does not belong to one special group, but she has a few very close friends. She doesn't like to boss, but she will take over any assignment and do it well. She meets competition well. She is very conscientious about all school rules. She is never tardy and has been absent only once this year. The teacher said that he has never seen anyone cross Connie or had her reported for anything. She scored somewhat below average on an intelligence test given in the fourth grade.

✺✺✺✺✺

This girl had low peer scores in one of the lowest of the schools socioeconomically. Her description resembles that of least-liked children of other ethnic backgrounds. Her family situation was very disturbed. In comparing her with some of the other cases being described here, it would seem that the low-choice scores were not primarily a function of her ethnic background.

Linda (fifth grade) is a thin girl, one of the tallest in the class, with noticeably long arms. She is always neat and clean in appearance, but has a rather awkward gait — slightly pigeon-toed. Linda talks constantly, and if no one is around, she just talks or mumbles to herself, which often gets her into trouble. She probably does not talk this way to show off, but rather this seems to be a nervous or emotional condition and method of release to her.

Linda has average intelligence. Quite often she gets into arguments with the other children. In many ways her thinking seems more mature than some of the others in the class. This is especially so in her attitude and behavior toward boys which she seems to have gotten from an older sister. When corrected she becomes angry and pouts. Linda has friends among the lower group and is accepted by those who are also unliked or unaccepted. Linda has contact with boys and quite often there have been reports of boys striking her, chasing her home, etc. The teacher felt that some of the girls might be a little jealous of Linda because of her more mature thinking and ideas about boys, but that there are other children who dislike her primarily because she causes disturbances in class. They do not show overt hostility toward her, however, but certainly they tend to ignore her.

The family has been known to the school for some time. The mother has been hospitalized a number of times and has just recently been released. During this time, the father is left with the responsibility of caring for the children, which is quite difficult for him. As a result Linda and her sister's attendance has been quite poor. Their traumatic and unstable home life has left its mark on Linda and her sister. They try to help each other, and when one is ill and needs to stay home, the other one will remain home to care for her. Consequently both have had a lot of absences.

⚹⚹⚹⚹⚹⚹

This boy had high peer scores in a low SES school in which more than one-fourth of the pupils were of his ethnic background. We also have a qualitative description for him at the sixth-grade level. By that time he had transferred to a parochial school in which the proportion of pupils similar in ethnic background was definitely smaller.

Thomas (in third grade) is dark, rather small, not always too neat, a little below average in cleanliness. His intelligence is a little above average. He is, perhaps, one of the smarter boys in the room. He is a good athlete and a storyteller.

On the playground he joins in and likes to play. He is a leader, one of the first to be chosen, and is dependable. Some of these characteristics hold over to the classroom too. He behaves well, is responsible, and always has his work in on time. With others he relates easily and well. No one ever seems to report him for getting into difficulty. With the teacher he has a good adjustment. He does not ask many questions as he seems to be bright enough to go ahead on his own. This year he has improved somewhat on his self-discipline. The children like him and choose him early due to his dependability, brightness, and ability as a leader.

The family is not too well known to the teacher, although she is aware that Thomas does not mind too well at home. It is a small family. The mother is cooperative with the school.

⚹⚹⚹⚹⚹⚹

Thomas (in sixth grade) is a nice-looking boy, small for his age. He's one year older than his classmates, but about the same size. He's very well built. He has a very pleasant personality, always has a smile, and seems in a good mood. His Mexican background seems to be of little or no significance in his social acceptance. He is a very willing worker, sees a task through, and is very democratic. On the playground he's physically quite capable and is distinguished by his fair play. In the classroom, there's a positive attitude too. Sometimes he gets into a little mischief, but this is not usual. He has a good relationship with others and a very positive relationship with the teacher. He's somewhat forward but very well mannered. He has matured a great deal emotionally this year. Classmates' reactions to him — he's very well accepted because of his fairness and his keen sense of feeling for others. He has fairly good academic ability. His family is close-knit. Mother remarried several years ago. There are older children from the first marriage and then two or three little children from the second marriage. The stepfather wishes the older children to be known by his name, and he has been very critical of the school when there was a question of the legality of doing this. There seems to be a good deal of attachment between Tom and his stepfather. It is also a well-disciplined home. Tom has duties there which he must perform before he can play or go off on his own to do other things.

〰〰〰

This girl had high peer scores in a school in the lowest quartile socioeconomically in which a majority of the other pupils had ethnic backgrounds similar to hers. In spite of some family problems, she seems to get along well.

Juanita (fifth grade) is average in size. She's very neat, very well dressed, and well groomed. She's a happy, smiling girl. She stands out as the best worker among the girls in the room. She's a good reader, is good in arithmetic, and her writing can be very good. Her weakness, if any, is lack of self-confidence. She seems to be afraid of going ahead because she might make a mistake, asks unnecessary questions, wants to do things exactly as the teacher wants. On the playground she's a leader. Girls look up to her and follow along. She's also a leader in the class. She's polite, although she sometimes seems a little bit of a smarty during lunch.

Around the room she's very helpful, volunteers to help other children and the teacher. She has an easy relationship with teachers and other adults. Changes this year are just general growth and maturation. She acts more like older children than like the little girl that she was in the fall.

Classmates accept her, choose her as a leader, think she's very nice. They cooperate with her and respond to her leadership. The reasons are that they've seen her work and know it's good, and she's helpful to them. She's a happy girl.

Her mother has been divorced and recently married. The mother is expecting a child now and Juanita seems pleased. She has two older sisters. She seems to be very close to her grandmother and talks much of her, likes to be with her.

〰〰〰

This girl had low peer scores in the same school as that of the preceding pupil. There is a suggestion that her family may have been migrant, and that her schooling had been more irregular than that of most of the others described here.

At first Lucia's (sixth grade) appearance was pretty messy, her hair was untidy, and she was not very clean, but now her appearance is better. She is a slight child, nice looking. She's individualized by being rather naïve. She's far behind the others in schoolwork and does not seem to realize it. She seems to have no sense of how to behave, chews gum, has poor study habits, cannot stick to a task. She's very poor academically, about two grades behind. There seems to be all weaknesses, and there are few strengths. She doesn't play with the group, but goes off by herself on the swings. She just doesn't seem to get involved with other children.

In the classroom and in school she's not very dependable and the other children check on her. She has a somewhat hostile attitude toward the teacher. She resents criticism and help, although she has seemed more appreciative recently of the teacher helping her and she is trying to do better work. Teacher notes some improvement in schoolwork since she was put back on easier material that she could handle better. As a strength she hands in nice neat spelling papers.

Classmates are pretty much indifferent to her although she has two friends, very different girls. The reason for this is that Lucia is not very aggressive. She doesn't apply herself, she doesn't do what's expected.

Mother did not come for conference, but she did come to the office to see the principal on one occasion. She seemed sweet and kind. The family went to a southern state for several weeks almost two months ago. The father went to look for work, so the children were out of this school, and the teachers of both children have wondered if they actually were enrolled in schools there since it seemed that they had made little or no progress in work during the time they were gone.

⁂

This boy had low peer scores in the same school as that of the two preceding girls. As sometimes happened in this sample, the ethnic background of the mother is different from that of the father, on whom the classification is based. There is some conflict within the family, which is not necessarily typical of the situation. The personality characteristics of the boy are not unlike those of low children from other backgrounds.

Mark (fifth grade) is a large, nice-looking boy, usually quite clean, dress is average for the group. He tends to be something of a bully, but less now than earlier in the year. He likes to be the center of attraction, but uses force to get attention. His best work is in arithmetic and he's very weak in reading. He's not very good at getting along with other children.

On the playground he makes excuses if he misses the ball or anything else goes wrong. He has average ability and coordination. In the classroom he makes alibis and excuses for his failures. He obeys the rules, sometimes quite nicely. Sometimes he's noisy but is usually well behaved. He has to be reminded of how to treat others, but can work well with them if he tries. Sometimes they ignore him, thinking he is incapable, especially in relation to schoolwork. He responds quite well toward the teacher. He tries most of the time. His inability to read influences everything he does. He thinks he can't do this or that. He likes to do extra things in the room and is cooperative with the teacher. He gets along better with the children than he had earlier. There are not as many arguments. He doesn't alibi as much as he used to.

Classmates know that he wants to be liked and to be a leader on the playground, but they think he doesn't have the ability. They don't choose him for leader, but they will choose him for their team. Mark has no special friends, but he goes along with the group.

Mother came to school for both conferences. She made some excuses for Mark's absences. She is a pleasant person. The father was not seen by the teacher. The school social worker is acquainted with the family and worked with the mother, particularly in regard to Mark's lack of interest in school, poor attendance, and poor productivity. The father is Mexican, the mother is not; there are family difficulties. Mother has indicated that there is little or no cooperation from the father or understanding of her problems with the children. He leaves raising the children entirely up to her, while he goes about seeking his own pleasures.

The family's poor school attendance seems due in part to the way the family is managed; sometimes they've had no alarm clock. There is no cooperation between father and mother. It seems as though the mother is pretty much bogged down with young chil-

dren. The younger children and a mentally retarded preschool
child have had many illnesses. The father has been out of work at
times, so lack of money was a problem. The mother has kept Mark
and his older brother, who is a much more responsible boy, at
home to babysit.

6

~~~~~

Peer Status and
Background Factors

Three somewhat different approaches were followed to determine the
relationship between family characteristics and the peer status of the
children involved. The first makes use of the structured interview information which had been obtained in Minnesota about children and
their families. Frequencies of occurrence of different family characteristics are examined for pupils who were high, average, and low in peer
status; a breakdown is also made by socioeconomic status of the families. A second approach makes use of an open-end questionnaire for a
sample of 685 Texas pupils, again comparing children of high and low
peer status. The information obtained is oriented more toward negative (a history of being on welfare, a criminal history, and a history of
moving around with unusual frequency) than toward positive factors.
The third approach makes use of a questionnaire for structured interviews concerning family background factors which was administered
to a sample of 59 Texas families. This yields results which are in harmony with those of the first two approaches.

AN ANALYSIS OF FAMILY INFORMATION
OBTAINED IN INTERVIEWS

The last part of the structured interview administered in Minnesota consisted of reports by school personnel of the particular strengths
and weaknesses of pupils' families. These were analyzed to get information on family background factors in relation to peer status. It was

realized that in some cases the teachers would have little information about their pupils' families, but it seemed worthwhile to get whatever information was available. Compared with the family descriptions present in case histories of good child guidance clinics (Roff, Mink, & Hinrichs, 1966), these are, of course, brief. However, the analysis did yield a significant amount of information for a substantial number of families, including many whose children are getting along well. Thus, the family information analyzed here comes from a broader sample than that from studies in which more intensive information is available, but which deal primarily with children who have problems of various types. Specific family information was given for over half of the children. The proportion of interviews with usable family information was approximately the same for schools at all socioeconomic levels, but was slightly lower for low-choice pupils.

Analysis of family information began with the development of appropriate descriptive categories. Statements were then placed in these categories for the three groups of children of high-, average-, or low-choice status. Classification was done by workers who had no knowledge of peer choice scores of the pupils whose interviews they were reading. (Of course, most of the interviews contained descriptions of the child's peer relationships and often gave some indication of the child's relative status.) Then the initial classification of comments was rechecked on the basis of the family information alone, by still other workers who had no knowledge of either the child's peer choice score or his nonfamily interview information.

Each category of family information was characterized as positive, neutral, or negative, according to its observed relation to peer status. Stated abstractly, the categories more or less agree with parental descriptions in the general child psychology literature. To give these general terms concrete meaning, sample family descriptions abstracted from the interviews are included in the discussion that follows. In many cases these offer a sharply contrasting picture of "good" and "poor" parental practices as they relate to the social adjustment of children. Again SES divisions used here refer to schools and not to individual family units; it is, of course, possible for a family to be somewhat higher or lower in SES than the average family in its neighborhood. Since the sample for which family information was available is smaller than those used in earlier analyses, a division on the basis of socioeconomic level was made only into halves rather than into the quartiles or octiles which have been used in some other analyses. Table 17 presents comparisons of family information with peer status (low, middle, high), by ses.

Table 17. Positive, Neutral, and Negative Family Factors for Low-, Middle-, and High-Choice Children, Teacher Interview Sample

	Percentage in Peer Status Group		
	Low	Middle	High
Descriptive Category	(N = 581)	(N = 305)	(N = 317)
Positive			
Family is close, stable, secure, cohesive, warm, happy, does things together, etc.			
Upper half ses	14	45	57
Lower half ses	8	24	42
Parents are interested in their children, show concern, care about them, want them to have advantages, etc.			
Upper half ses	19	47	47
Lower half ses	15	27	40
Parents cooperate with the school, are active in pta, come for conferences, act on teacher's suggestions, etc.			
Upper half ses	23	41	41
Lower half ses	12	28	39
Neutral			
Mother is employed full or part-time			
Upper half ses	17	13	21
Lower half ses	16	24	18
Parents are separated or divorced			
Upper half ses	11	5	3
Lower half ses	20	20	15
No father in the home, mother is not remarried			
Upper half ses	7	4	3
Lower half ses	12	15	11
Child has a stepparent			
Upper half ses	2	2	3
Lower half ses	10	7	7
Parents are overprotective			
Upper half ses	7	1	1
Lower half ses	6	5	6
Parent or other person in the home is physically handicapped or seriously ill			
Upper half ses	3	6	1
Lower half ses	5	3	3
Child lives with someone other than parents			
Upper half ses	2	3	1
Lower half ses	6	4	2

Table 17 — continued

Descriptive Category	Percentage in Peer Status Group		
	Low (N = 581)	Middle (N = 305)	High (N = 317)
Negative			
Family is unstable, tense, unhappy, has many problems, conflict of authority, fighting, etc.			
Upper half SES	16	3	4
Lower half SES	21	10	5
Parents don't supervise, are indifferent, unconcerned, lack authority, lack control, too busy for children, children are left alone frequently, don't care what children do, etc.			
Upper half SES	13	4	1
Lower half SES	18	8	3
Parents are uncooperative with the school, blame the teachers, are critical, defensive, interfere with the teachers, habitually fail to keep conference appointments, fail to follow teachers' suggestions, etc.			
Upper half SES	15	2	3
Lower half SES	17	6	1
Family is financially deprived, on relief, has a hard time making ends meet, receives ADC, income is much below average for neighborhood, etc.			
Upper half SES	10		
Lower half SES	12	7	4
Factors Infrequently Mentioned Showing Possible Negative Trends			
Parents are rejecting, want to put child in boarding home, resent the child, favor his siblings, etc.			
Upper half SES	6		
Child is spoiled, overindulged, given everything he wants, etc.			
Upper half SES	3	1	
Lower half SES	4	1	1
Parents are ambivalent, inconsistent, etc.			
Upper half SES	2		
Lower half SES	4	1	
Parent(s) are (were) in trouble with the law, in prison, etc.			
Lower half SES	4	2	1
Parent is mentally ill, seeing a psychiatrist, had a nervous breakdown, has been in a state hospital, etc.			
Upper half SES	1		
Lower half SES	3	4	1
Parent is of low intelligence, not too bright, etc.			
Upper half SES	1	3	
Lower half SES	4	3	

Positive Factors. Three discriminable sets of items have been included under positive factors. These are unquestionably correlated. All three discriminate between families of high– and low–peer status children at the .01 level or better. The sets of differentiating characteristics (family harmony and cohesiveness, positive interest in children, and cooperation with school) are similar to factors which have emerged in formal factor analyses of family variables beginning with Roff (1949). The largest difference between the upper and lower SES groups among the families with high–peer status children occurs in family stability, cohesiveness, warmth, and so forth. On the category of interest in their children the difference between the two SES groups is not so large. On the parents' cooperation with school, PTA, and so forth, it is interesting to note that among families with high–peer status children, there is little difference between the two SES groups, whereas the difference between upper and lower SES groups for families with children of low–peer status is marked. Typical descriptions in positive categories are as follows.

   a. Family is stable, secure, cohesive, and so forth

❧❧❧❧❧

A very supporting family that does things together, making frequent trips and having family experiences. They provide many opportunities for the children. The standards of the family are high, but they do give freedom to Frank. There are no known weaknesses.

❧❧❧❧❧

The mother participates in activities involving the children and gives good care. She gives assistance freely to Jane and her siblings, shows keen interest and insight in the children, and involves them in many activities that are good for them.

❧❧❧❧❧

Gloria comes from an excellent family. The parents are completely thrilled with her. They have great fun teasing each other. She has a little brother in kindergarten, and they are a very close-knit family. They do many cultural things as a family such as taking trips, reading books and magazines, and listening to music.

b. Parents concerned about and interested in children

~~~~~

The mother shows an interest in children and comes to school when Herbert has a part in a program. This is an Aid to Dependent Children family, but the mother seems to manage well. The children are always well cared for and well groomed.

~~~~~

The mother came for a conference and worked with a school immunization clinic. She is much interested in Pam's classroom achievement. The father went with the group on an airplane ride.

c. Parents active in PTA and cooperative with school

~~~~~

Roxanne comes from a very fine family as far as school cooperation is concerned. Both parents come to PTA and are very interested in their children's achievement.

~~~~~

Larry's parents are among the very best PTA members; his father has been president and his mother has been very helpful and willing on committees. They have good feelings toward school.

Neutral Factors. Descriptive characteristics included in this category are those in which the differences in family situation between low-, average-, and high-choice children are either not significant or small. Most of these refer to factual items such as the mother's employment, separation or divorce, and parents' physical handicap or illness. Illustrative comments are not necessary for these. Although some might show a technically significant difference if the sample were greatly increased in size or if a sample of a different character, such as a clinic sample, were used, they would still be rather ineffective items in separating low-, average-, and high-choice children.

Negative Factors. Families described as unstable, tense, unhappy, and so on (the opposite of positive factor *a*) clearly differentiate between high– and low–peer status children, but show less difference between upper and lower SES. Similarly, parental lack of interest, indifference, and neglect discriminate between families with upper– and lower–peer status children in both SES groups; so does the factor "uncooperative with school." A fourth factor, economic deprivation, differentiates between the families with high– and low–peer status children, but has no parallel among the positive factors, possibly because economic adequacy did not receive much mention. The 10 per cent of the families among the upper SES group which drew this comment were all families with low–peer status children, whereas those in the bottom SES group were about equally divided between low–, average–, and high–peer status children. It should be noted that the economic inadequacy factor includes not only absolute measures, such as being on relief, but also relative measures such as "income is much below average for neighborhood." Concrete illustrations from the school information are given below.

a. Family is unstable, and so forth

❧❧❧❧❧

Julie's parents have been separated for a number of years. In fact, there have been two divorces. Mother seems to love Julie, but at times is annoyed by her demands for attention, which she is sometimes unable to handle.

❧❧❧❧❧

Virginia's mother seems to project blame on others. She is the mother of one illegitimate child, has been married three times, and is definitely a walking paranoid who is in constant trouble with the authorities, welfare, and the law. On more than one occasion she has been called to court for possible child neglect. It is an almost impossible situation with this mother. The current father is nothing but a vegetable in many ways. He sought a mother figure, and found it in this domineering, sick woman.

❧❧❧❧❧

Ed has a stormy home life. His mother remarried and now is having marital problems with the stepfather. Ed is the third of six children. They have moved frequently — this is his sixth school in six years of elementary school. Ed does not make his home difficulties known, and it is only of late that the mother has admitted to real physical abuses on the part of a drunken stepfather at times.

b. Parents unconcerned and uninterested in child

〰〰〰〰〰

Gail's mother relies heavily on her boyfriend, who is on the road during the week but present on weekends. Much of the disciplining is done by him. The mother finds it impossible to discipline and manage her children.

〰〰〰〰〰

Janet and her siblings have been eating lunch at the nearby high school cafeteria. Mother does not want to fix lunch for them. She is not critical of the school but is rather indifferent to it. Her attitude seems to be that her children have problems so she lives with them.

〰〰〰〰〰

Kay's mother seems to be slowly falling apart, and the father has taken to spending a lot of time away from home, drinking excessively. The neglect is now such that it is a real question whether the children should be removed from the family.

〰〰〰〰〰

Ralph's stepfather is involved in politics, and at election time the youngster gets very little attention as the mother is never home. The mother is extremely aggressive and seems to be more interested in her own needs and status than in the needs of her kids. She pays lip service to wanting the best for them but is not always able to follow through.

〰〰〰〰〰

Jacob comes from an extremely deprived family situation where there seems to be very little concern about the children and almost complete lack of supervision. At the present time he is being cared for by his grandmother. Jacob has often told his teacher of having not come home at night, and apparently no one inquired about him.

✌✌✌✌

Jean's mother is high strung, nervous, and on the defensive. In addition to general poor health, she had a back injury and had to have surgery. She has been working long hours, leaving her children unsupervised. This mother has not given Jean any help with her schoolwork and appears to be involved in many personal problems.

c. Parents uncooperative with school

✌✌✌✌

Mother seems to enjoy the fights at school more than Luanne and her sister do. She usually says that there is prejudice, and she calls many names and so forth. The girls seem to enjoy having their mother settle their difficulties.

✌✌✌✌

Debby's mother does not do much to cooperate with the school. She does not interfere, but she certainly doesn't participate or give a great deal of herself. Neither is she too careful about attendance.

✌✌✌✌

The parents project all of Clifton's problems upon the school, using many excuses such as that the school put him in an easy book when he should have been in a hard one. The parents' attitude since he started school was that he was a very bright boy who could do no wrong. In fact, the parents have sabotaged the efforts of the school to help Clifton. They have not allowed him to like his teachers or to cooperate with school programs.

✌✌✌✌

Brad's mother is extremely antagonistic and hostile to school. She feels that her children have been picked on. When she talked to school personnel she was not even in a frame of mind that she could accept any direction in regard to the children. In fact, she usually had a very intense temper display, using foul language.

d. Family financially deprived

⨯⨯⨯⨯⨯⨯

Mother receives Aid for Dependent Children for the three oldest and social security for the youngest three. She is a very poor manager and is always in debt; consequently Lola and her family have moved around a great deal.

⨯⨯⨯⨯⨯⨯

There is a poor physical environment in Harry's home; low economic conditions, improper diet, and lack of food — often no breakfast.

⨯⨯⨯⨯⨯⨯

Carl's father remains employed, which is a decided family strength, but his livelihood is not really sufficient for his many children. Actual physical surroundings are bare and sparse and there is sometimes not enough food and insufficient clothing.

Finally a set of factors are listed which show possible negative trends with respect to children's peer status, but are mentioned so infrequently as to appear to play a minor role in the total situation. These include rejecting parents (parental rejection was counted only when it was obviously indicated and was omitted when based only on such clinically oriented interpretations as "the mother shows so much overprotection that it is rejection"), statements that the child is spoiled, statements that discipline is inconsistent, and statements that the parents had been in trouble with the law, were mentally ill, or were of low intelligence. These have been mentioned here primarily because of the attention they have received from other research workers.

AN OPEN-END QUESTIONNAIRE EXPLORING
FAMILY ADJUSTMENT

The aim of the study described here was to use a somewhat different approach to family adjustment factors that would discriminate between children who are accepted and children who are rejected by their peers. The majority of subjects were selected on the basis of first-year LM – LL scores as high, middle (within SD above and below the mean), and low. However, since peer scores were available for two years, some cases were added which were high in one year and low in the other. Using the mean combined peer-teacher score for both years and splitting at the mean of 5.0 (to distinguish high from low children), there were 326 boys (96 high and 230 low) and 359 girls (117 high and 242 low) in the final sample of 685 pupils.

SES level was determined by ordering the eighty-two participating schools on the basis of median number of years of education completed by adults twenty-five and over for the appropriate census units based on 1960 census data. The schools were divided into thirds, and each pupil was classified as high, middle, or low in SES according to the position of his school. Most of the sample came from school districts in fairly large Texas cities; a minority came from two smaller Texas communities.

An open-end questionnaire was designed to cover nine general areas of possible family adjustment problems, and arrangements were made with the school coordinators in seven Texas school districts to obtain this information. Each coordinator was furnished a form for each child in his sample and was asked to obtain available information in any of the following categories: psychiatric history for any member; welfare history; history of criminal or deviant behavior; significant medical history and/or physical handicap; family structure — divorce, separation, or other major disruption in the child's parental family; a history of frequent moves; unusual or atypical parental occupational history (e.g., unemployment, marginal worker, father travels, overseas); and unusual parental educational background (e.g., parents are illiterate, foreign language is spoken in the home). The peer status of these children was not indicated on the questionnaires. The school coordinators were requested to include only information obtained from sources which could be independently verified.

A total of 732 comments was received for the 685 children in the sample. The resulting comments were grouped into the original categories and several additional subcategories. Each comment was classified with respect to the family members principally involved (father, mother, sibling, and/or subject). A brief description illustrating typical comments classified under each of the major categories is presented below.

a. Psychiatric history or peculiar behavior on the part of any family member

The whole family is emotionally disturbed — possibly due to the mother's instability.

The father is not well balanced — he ran away, has been in mental institution.

The mother had a nervous breakdown last year.

The father has received psychiatric treatment — seems to have recovered.

b. Welfare history

This is a broken home — the father left some time ago. The mother and children are on welfare.

This child has received special help from a welfare agency for a speech defect. Her parents are divorced and her stepfather unemployed.

Her family has been on relief since she was born.

This family has the record for longest term of relief in the county.

c. Criminal history

The father has been in penitentiary for theft.

The mother has been arrested.

The father has been arrested on more than one occasion. His behavior is not good.

d. Family structure: divorce, separation, or other major disruptions in the family

The mother has not divorced all her husbands, but has had four or five.

The two children and their mother have three different names.

The parents have been separated but are now living together.

The mother has been married five times. She drinks heavily. The father and mother are separated. The mother left home and now lives in California. The child lives with her father. There is a separation in the family; the mother has lived with two or three different men.

e. History of moving

This family has moved a lot because the father is in service. The pupil has attended school in Europe.

They change their home address often, and change schools within the city.

This child has been in three schools in this city during the past two years.

The family moves often — three times in the past three years. The family moves away, then back about once a year.

f. Exceptional educational backgrounds: illiterate, bilingual, etc.

This is a bilingual family.

The father and mother are both almost illiterate.

The family is bilingual and has low mentality.

g. Unusual or atypical occupational history

The father is unemployed most of the time.

The father has no regular employment, but works irregularly in oil fields.

The father is unemployed for periods so there is little income.

The father is a marginal worker. He is unemployed for long periods and earns practically no income.

Table 18. Percentage of Adverse Comments about Family History by Peer Status (Upper or Lower Half) and SES

Category	Low SES		Middle SES		High SES	
	Lower Half[a]	Upper Half[b]	Lower Half[c]	Upper Half[d]	Lower Half[e]	Upper Half[f]
Psychiatric history	2	3	5	1	7	
Welfare history	11	1	11	1		
Criminal history	10		10			
Family structure	27	11	15	8	7	5
Family mobility	9	1	10	1	6	
Educational history	7		7		2	
Occupational history	11	5	29	7	9	5

[a] $N = 105$.   [b] $N = 102$.   [c] $N = 179$.
[d] $N = 71$.   [e] $N = 88$.   [f] $N = 40$.

Results. The relative frequencies of adverse comments in the several family background categories were examined in relation to SES and peer scores. The results (Tables 18 and 19) show a consistent trend for adverse comments to be associated with low peer status, as summarized below.

Psychiatric or peculiar behavior — this category was associated with peer status for high and middle, but not low, SES.

Welfare history — comments on this item did not appear for high SES, but were related to peer status for middle and low SES.

Criminal history — this category was associated with low peer status for middle and low SES.

Table 19. Frequency Distribution of Adverse Comments about Family History, Combined First- and Second-Year Peer-Teacher Scores

Category	Low Choice[a] N	Low Choice[a] %	Middle Choice[b] N	Middle Choice[b] %	High Choice[c] N	High Choice[c] %	Total[d] N	Total[d] %
Psychiatric history								
Father	6	2.5	2	.7			8	1.2
Mother	4	1.7	3	1.0			7	1.0
Sibling	3	1.2	3	1.0			6	.9
Child	3	1.2					3	.4
Welfare history	42	17.4	14	4.8			56	8.2
Criminal history, parent or child	17	7.1	3	1.0			20	2.9
Family structure								
Death of family member	10	4.1	12	4.2	3	1.9	25	3.6
Parents separated	23	9.5	11	3.8	4	2.6	38	5.5
Parents divorced	20	8.3	15	5.2	6	3.9	41	6.0
No adult male in the home	6	2.5	2	.7	1	.6	9	1.3
Child lives with other than parent(s)	16	6.6	10	3.5	2	1.3	28	4.1
Family mobility								
Child changed schools often	10	4.1	1	.4			11	1.6
Family moves often	20	8.3	16	5.5			36	5.2
Education history of parents								
Illiterate	7	2.9	12	4.2			19	2.8
Less than high school education	4	1.7	5	1.7			9	1.3
Bilingual home	13	5.4	13	4.5	2	1.3	28	4.1
Occupational or work history								
Frequent or current unemployment	16	6.6	13	4.5	1	.6	30	4.4
Father is marginal/ itinerant worker	6	2.5	10	3.5	1	.6	17	2.5
Mother supports family	4	1.7	11	3.8	2	1.3	17	2.5

[a]$N = 241.$ [b]$N = 289.$
[c]$N = 155.$ [d]$N = 685.$

Family structure — in Table 19 disrupted parental relations occur almost twice as often in low– as in high–peer status groups of middle SES, and nearly three times as often in low–peer status groups of low SES. For high SES, the percentage difference between high– and low–peer status children is only slight.

Family mobility — comments on this category, like those pertaining to welfare and education history, were highly associated with peer status.

Educational history — the relationship between adverse comments concerning parents' education and peer status of the child was consistent across SES levels in that no comments were made on children with above average peer scores.

Occupational history — the association between peer status and father's employment history was consistent. In this study, most of the families with the father in military service were in the middle- and high-SES schools, but children from these families tended to be relatively low in peer status. Three factors may account for their low peer status: (a) the periodic absence of fathers from home, (b) the discrepancy between the social status of the family and the SES level of the school that the child attends, and (c) the possibility that the families may have moved a good deal more often than average.

FOLLOW-UP STUDY OF FAMILY PATHOLOGY USING A STRUCTURED QUESTIONNAIRE

The results of the preceding study were used as the basis of a questionnaire for structured interviews concerning family background factors of a small group of Texas children for whom peer scores were available. This structured questionnaire required a definite yes or no answer for every item.

The final sample included 59 families: 34 high– and 25 low–peer status children, based on average LM – LL scores for the first two years. A larger sample had been planned, but the interviews proved more time-consuming than expected, since it was necessary to consult five or six sources for each child. Interviewers obtained the information for various parts of the questionnaire from community sources, including school records. The results were tabulated in relation to scores on the combined peer-teacher rating as shown in Appendix Table 6.

Adverse family history comments were associated with peer acceptance-rejection in much the same manner as in the study based on the open-end questionnaire. Although a multivariate analysis of these data would be appropriate with a larger sample, this was not considered desirable because of the relatively small sample size. Even conventional tests of significance have been omitted here, in line with the rule of thumb that unsatisfactory results may be obtained in a chi-square setting with cells less than five and with one degree of freedom.

Parents' health — the presence of one or more serious illnesses was scored for father and for mother. The response frequencies were in the expected direction.

Child's medical history — none of the four scores for visual impairment, hearing impairment, speech impairment, and a history of serious illness occurred frequently enough to evaluate separately. Analysis of the responses in this category showed some relation of speech, hearing, and possibly vision problems to peer rejection.

Social history of the family — incidence of death, separation, and divorce were included in this category. Results in the same direction as those of the open-end questionnaire were found for all items but "death of family member."

Parental attitudes — two school-related items, "Do not cooperate with school" and "Unconcerned about school absence," agreed with similar findings described above.

Psychiatric history or "need for psychiatric examination" — more low than high children had a family member with either a psychiatric history or judged in need of psychiatric examination by an informant.

Welfare history — some 44 per cent of the families of low and 6 per cent of high choice children were reported to have received welfare aid. This is the largest difference among this group of items.

Criminal history — this category included reports of criminal behavior on the part of a parent or delinquent behavior on the part of the child. It differed in the expected direction.

Family mobility — no families of high children and 24 per cent of the families with low children were reported as having moved often.

Education history of parents — over half of the fathers and mothers of the high group and 12 per cent of the mothers of the low group had completed high school. This is in line with other results relating to SES.

Occupational history — responses indicating that the father was unemployed, often unemployed, had difficulty holding a job, and so on differentiated between low- and high-choice groups.

The responses for this questionnaire were grouped to yield two scores: Family Background Problems and Unfavorable Parental Attitudes. The results of this procedure are shown in Table 20. Both sets

Table 20. High- and Low-Choice Children with Scores above and below Median for Family Questionnaire

Scores	Low Choice		High Choice	
	N	%	N	%
Family background problems				
Below median	4	16	27	79
Above median	21	84	7	21
Unfavorable parental attitudes				
Below median	7	28	31	91
Above median	18	72	3	9

of items clearly differentiate between the parents of high– and low–peer status children. This further corroborates the importance of the family as an influence on children's peer status.

7

✖✖✖✖✖

Family and Personality Characteristics and Peer Status

The data presented in this chapter have been selected by the authors from a doctoral thesis by Cox (1966) who was part of the project for several years. His study undertook an independent investigation within the general framework of the main peer relations study in order to determine the relationships to one another and to the child's peer-choice scores of socioeconomic status, family background, parental child-rearing attitudes and practices, and characteristics of the child. No attempt has been made to cover everything he reports; the interpretations presented here are those of the authors, and Dr. Cox should not be held responsible for them.

The main study obtained converging results from several approaches that implicated the child's family as a significant influence in peer acceptance-rejection. Cox attempted to bring some of the more salient family factors into sharper focus. From an extensive range and number of relevant biological, cultural, familial, and social factors, Cox selected several for study on the basis of their relation to past research and because they appear to represent pivotal aspects of several related classes of variables that can be combined into a conceptually related network. Such a network was hypothesized among four sets of variables: (a) *family background and social factors,* which reflect parents' socioeconomic and educational level and hence the level of ease, comfort, enlightenment, and perhaps goals for the children of the family; (b) *parental child-rearing attitudes and practices,* which were assumed to influence the personality development of the children;

(c) *characteristics of the child,* such as sociability, self-concept, and intelligence, which seemed to be focal in peer relations; and (d) *peer acceptance-rejection.*

Several of the linkages in the hypothesized network of relationships have received extensive empirical attention. Others appear to have been largely ignored at the empirical level, although sometimes mentioned in theoretical formulations. The relevant literature has been reviewed at length by Cox (1966). Briefly, reports of empirical research concerning these four categories of variables indicated the following: First, social (economic and educational) level of the family has been related to factors in each of the other three sets of variables described above. Research emphasizing generally favorable effects of high SES and educational level has been extensive, and the results appear to be remarkably consistent. Second, parental attitudes and child-rearing practices have been found to be related to children's personality, behavior patterns, and adjustment. The research in this area has been less extensive, and the results appear more difficult to generalize. In general, loving and accepting parental attitudes and behavior have been associated with well-adjusted children. Third, many investigations have shown that a child's sociometric choice status is positively related to his favorable personality characteristics, intelligence, and various measures of good adjustment to home and school situations.

In the main study, no self-report instruments of any kind were administered to the pupils. Some information about parents of the children was obtained from school personnel, particularly in Minnesota, but no interviewing or questioning of the families themselves was done. However, a substantial number of studies have compared the results of personality inventories with choice status (Dahlke, 1953; Grossman & Wrighter, 1948; Guinouard & Rychlak, 1962; Sewell & Haller, 1959; Ullmann, 1957; Young & Cooper, 1944). These studies have indicated that there is some, but not a high, relationship between self-report scores and scores resulting from peer nominations.

Cox contributed information resulting from the active cooperation of a set of parents of pupils for whom peer scores were available, which supplements both the main study and the already existing studies of various aspects of peer status in the literature. A number of choice-status studies have used information about the parents, such as one or more of the classic triad of indicators of SES (parental education, income, and occupation of father) which can be obtained without much cooperation from the families involved (Davis, 1957; Elkins, 1958; Grossman & Wrighter, 1948; Hardy, 1937; Neugarten, 1946). It is well established that in schools which have not been too highly stratified on socioeconomic status, there is positive relationship between SES of the parents and choice status of their children. On the other hand, it is very hard to find studies in which the parents have cooperated systematically over quite a wide area. Cox's study is novel in that a vigorous attempt was made to obtain detailed information from both parents and children about parental attitudes and practices in child rearing for comparison with childhood peer status.

METHOD

Data Collection. The total data collection schedule produced information on 175 variables concerning home, parents, and children (Cox, 1966); not all of these are included here. Since the number of variables exceeded the size of the sample, and because many were highly interrelated, a strategy was devised for data reduction prior to analysis. Several methods were employed to develop pooled or composite scores that represented the original battery without substantial loss of meaning. In order to eliminate bias, the measures in each conceptual set were developed before examining relationships across any of the sets. The final, reduced battery consists of twenty-nine measures which represent twelve concepts in the following four major areas:

a. Family Background

Social level (as measured by family economic level, years of education of the father, and years of education of the mother)

Adverse family factors (as measured by a tension index, an unweighted composite of seventeen items thought to be symptomatic of family stress; information was obtained from the mother by use of an interview schedule)

b. Parents' Child-Rearing Attitudes and Practices (Concepts and measures adopted from Roe & Siegelman 1963). Five scores were obtained: Child's rating of father, child's rating of mother, mother's rating of herself, father's rating of himself, and a measure of the difference between the child's ratings of his father and mother for several scales, including the three listed here.

Loving-rejecting (as measured by summed standard scores for three Roe-Siegelman scales, "Loving," "Rejecting," and "Neglecting")

Casual-demanding (as measured by summed standard scores for four Roe-Siegelman scales, "Casual," "Demanding," "Symbolic-Love Punishment," and "Direct-Object Punishment")

Overt concern for the child (as measured by summed standard scores for three Roe-Siegelman scales "Protecting," "Symbolic-Love Reward," and "Direct-Object Reward")

c. Characteristics of the Child

Intelligence (as measured by the mean total scale IQ for two administrations of the California Test of Mental Maturity [Sullivan, Clark, & Teigs, 1957])

Self-concept (as measured by the total score of How I Feel About Myself [Piers & Harris, 1963])

Health problems (as measured by the "Health Index," an unweighted composite of twenty-seven items reported by the mother on the child's Medical History, an adaptation of the form used in the National Health survey, and six items reported by school personnel)

Socially effective behavior (as measured by positive trait pattern A, a factor score based on teachers' ratings on five bipolar traits [Cattell, 1963]; the positive poles were: "Nonaggressive, kind, considerate"; "conscientious, trust-worthy"; "adaptable, flexible"; "trustful of others"; and "cooperative, compliant, obedient")

Irritable, angry (as measured by negative trait pattern A, a factor score based on Bower's [1960] Class Play using nomination by peers: "gets angry and gets into many fights"; "bully who picks on smaller children"; "person

with a very bad temper"; "a very stubborn person")
Superego strength (as measured by positive trait pattern B,
a factor score based on teachers' ratings of four bipolar
Cattell traits, with positive poles defined by: "careful with
property of others"; "neat, tidy, orderly"; "persevering,
determined"; and "responsible"; and by negative trait
pattern B, based on peer nomination on a modified guess-
who procedure, the Class Play [Bower, 1960]; the following
items were included: "a hermit who doesn't like to be with
people"; "a neighbor who is careless with others' property";
"the laziest person in the world"; "a character who is a
sloppy dresser or very careless about how he or she looks";
and "a suspicious character who is not trusted by the others")

d. Peer Acceptance-Rejection Status (as measured by the four-
year average of the LM – LL scores).

Subjects. The children involved in the study were pupils of three
schools in a single Texas city in which about 700 pupils participated
in the main study for four consecutive years. The combined peer-
teacher score was used to define a high and a low group having scores
one or more SD's above or below the mean. If any of these were siblings, one subject was randomly selected so that no family would be
represented by more than one child in the study. This gave 125 pro-
spective subjects.

With the consent of the superintendent and the school board, personnel of the three participating schools described the project to these
families, and their cooperation was requested. It was explained to the
parents that careful steps would be taken to preserve the confidential-
ity of all information. Families of 25 prospects declined participation,
leaving 100 children approximately the same number of boys and girls
of high- and low-choice status, about equally distributed through the
sixth, seventh, and eighth grades. Only those families were included
for which children's ratings of both parents and mothers' self-ratings
were available. Since two divorced mothers were not living with their
families, it was not possible to obtain their self-ratings. One other child
was omitted. Thus, most of the data analyses in this chapter have an
N of 97 families. Fathers' self-ratings were available for only 75 of

these 97 families — 8 were divorced or not living with the family and 14 declined participation in the study. Of the unavailable fathers, 7 were parents of high-choice children, and 15 were fathers of low-choice children. Inasmuch as complete data were available for only 75 families, and data for mother and child for 97 families, analyses were made for these two samples. The missing fathers were, in a majority, cases from the low SES part of the sample.

The plan which was followed was to make one home visit and to hold two testing sessions for the parents. The children were tested during free time at school.

The use of high- and low-choice groups from the 700 pupils available, eliminating the substantial majority of middle cases, means that correlations of other variables with the peer group criterion differ from the correlations which would have been obtained if the entire sample had been used. They are not directly comparable with correlations reported in other chapters. For example, the correlation between TR and peer status was .57 using a carefully devised rating scale on our entire sample of children (p. 67). Using the high and low groups in this chapter's sample, this correlation rose to .75, as reported below. Similarly, the correlation between IQ and peer status is reported below as .54 for the sample of 97 children (see Table 21), whereas correlations reported in the literature are rarely much above .40, and commonly fall in the upper or middle .30's.

The lower the correlation of a variable with peer status, the less selection on peer status would result in a corresponding selection on a second variable. Thus, the variables reported below would have somewhat different amounts of selection, depending upon the size of their correlations with peer status. In spite of these limitations, tables of correlations among some of the variables listed above and correlations of these with peer status are reported, since some of the comparisons of these with each other are very interesting.

RESULTS

The 75-Family Sample. Table 21 presents the intercorrelations of fourteen variables, representing the four conceptual sets described above, for the 75 families for whom there were complete data. Of the

Table 21. Intercorrelations of Fourteen Variables from Four Conceptual Sets for (N = 75 Families) [a][b]

Measure	110	120	215	225	233	234	241	242	311	321	331	341	351
120	-47**												
215	23*	-31**											
225	21	-11	54**										
233	-28*	28*	-25*	-32**									
234	-4	15	-21	-12	43**								
241	-30**	37**	-34**	-12	-1	-4							
242	-26*	41**	-36**	-4	-7	1	44**						
311	53**	-38**	35**	29**	-6	-16	-21	-30**					
321	33*	-35**	52**	36**	-14	-13	-28*	-28*	44**				
331	-31**	45**	-53**	-32**	20	6	40**	27*	-28*	-41**			
341	28*	-33**	33**	26*	-15	-25*	-12	-23*	41**	39**	-30**		
351	30**	-31**	40**	29**	-15	-10	-23*	-29**	37**	35**	-42**	72**	
400	26*	-44**	48**	29**	-12	-7	-26*	-31**	53**	62**	-50**	57**	48**

[a] Decimals omitted.
[b] *100, Family background:* 110, social level; 120, adverse family factors; *200, child-rearing practices:* 215, loving-rejecting; 225, casual-demanding; 233, mother's overt concern, self-rating; 234, father's overt concern, self-rating; 241, parental disagreement, loving-rejecting; 242, parental disagreement, casual-demanding; *300, child's characteristics:* 311, IQ; 321, self-concept; 331, health problems; 341, positive trait pattern A, teacher rating; 351, positive trait pattern B, teacher rating; *400, peer acceptance-rejection* (LM — LL).
*$p < .05$. **$p < .01$.

91 correlation coefficients in this matrix, 66 were significantly greater than zero ($p<.05$) and in the direction expected according to hypothesized relationships, as set forth in detail by Cox (1966). Of the 25 nonsignificant coefficients, 19 involved the two measures of overt concern (Roe-Siegelman's factor O), which apparently failed to perform as expected; 4 others involved consensual casual-demanding, and 2 others involved parental disagreement (Loving-Rejecting). If the two measures of overt concern had been omitted, the yield of correlation coefficients significantly different from zero in Table 21 would have been 60 out of 66.

The 97-Family Sample. Table 22 presents the intercorrelations for 22 measures, arranged by sets, for the mothers and children in the 97-family sample. Of the 231 correlation coefficients in the matrix, 144 were significantly greater than zero in the expected direction. Of the 87 nonsignificant correlations, 47 involved three measures of overt concern. If these three measures had been omitted, the yield of correlation coefficients significantly different from zero would have been 129 out of 171.

DISCUSSION OF CORRELATION MATRICES

Family Background. The measure of *social level,* based on family income and parents' education, was expected to reflect the influence of SES and education on (a) parental knowledge, skill, understanding, values, and acceptance of a responsible role in parenthood; and (b) factors which contribute to tension and conflict, such as deprivation, financial strain, overcrowding, and the like. The correlations indicate that children of high social level families were at a marked advantage over those from low families. High social level was significantly correlated with low adverse family factors; loving rather than rejecting parental attitudes; casual rather than punishing or demanding mothers' attitudes, according to self-ratings but not otherwise; and agreement between parents in expressed child-rearing attitudes. In the children it was positively correlated with high IQ; positive self-concept; absence of serious health problems; personality trait patterns (as rated by teachers) reflecting outgoing, friendly, and considerate relations to others; high superego strength; and high peer acceptance.

Table 22. Intercorrelations of Twenty Variables from Four Conceptual Sets (N = 97 Families) [a][b]

Measure	110	120	211	212	213	221	222	223	231	232	233	311	321	322	331	341	351	342	352
120	-47**																		
211	24*	-26**																	
212	-36**	-23*	73**																
213	37**	-27**	26**	24*															
221	13	-15	39**	28**	26**														
222	15	-11	41**	40**	10	71**													
223	30**	-16	28**	36**	27**	29**	33**												
231	-6	-5	41**	25*	-11	-13	-6	3											
232	6	-4	29**	32**	-10	-18	-10	20*	72**										
233	-13	19	-12	-17	-13	-14	-7	-44**		3									
311	48**	-35**	42**	41**	21*	8	8	14	12	12	-2								
321	31*	-26**	56**	56**	21*	22*	32**	20*	17	7	-9	48**							
322	-26**	18	-47**	-46**	-19	-28**	-25*	14	-17	-11	18	-42**	-64**						
331	-31**	39**	-53**	-40**	-29**	-25*	-23*	-18	-12	-5	19	-35**	-48**	51**					
341	24*	-31**	32**	33**	36**	23*	19	26**	6	6	-21*	35**	43**	-39	-36**				
351	26**	-34**	40**	38**	32**	24*	25*	23*	7	8	-20*	38**	40**	-35**	-43**	73**			
342	-13	25*	-9	-23*	7	-6	-13	-17	11	-1	21*	-24*	-31**	38**	18	-33**	-15		
352	-27**	34**	-35**	-33**	-28**	-23*	-25*	-21*	-7	1	20*	-44**	-52**	47**	52**	-55**	-67**	21*	
411	27**	-47**	54**	38**	27**	25*	25*	17	22*	13	-6	54**	61**	-49**	-53**	56**	54**	-23*	-64**

[a] Decimals omitted.

[b] 100, Family background: 110, social level; 120, family tension; 200, child-bearing practices: 211, loving-rejecting, C rating F; 212, loving-rejecting, C rating M; 213, loving-rejecting, M rating C; 221, casual-demanding, C rating F; 222, casual-demanding, C rating M; 223, casual-demanding, M rating C; 231, father's overt-concern, C rating F; 232, mother's overt-concern, C rating M; 233, mother's overt-concern, M rating C; 300, child's characteristics: 311, IQ; 321, self-concept; 322, child's problems; 331, health index; 341, positive trait pattern A (TR); 351, positive trait pattern B (TR); 342, negative pattern A (peer); 352, negative pattern B (peer); 400, peer acceptance-rejection (LM−LL): 411, loving-demanding.

*$p<.05$.   **$p<.01$.

The scale developed to measure *adverse family factors* included a number of items judged to be situationally diagnostic of stressful and tension-producing family situations. With only minor exceptions, the correlates of this scale conformed to theoretical expectations. Examination of the correlates of adverse family factors (Tables 21 and 22) shows that this variable was markedly related with measures of parental disagreement and also with the child's self-concept, health problems, personality trait ratings, and peer status. In general, these data suggest that some unfavorable conditions and events disrupt harmony in the family and produce tensions which manifest themselves at every level in the matrix of relationships.

Parental Child-Rearing Practices and Attitudes. A pattern similarity analysis strongly supported the definition of an attitude dimension of *loving-rejecting,* which is stable across groups of differing age and sex. The correlations of the measure of loving-rejecting (Tables 21 and 22) indicate that it was the best single measure of the parental attitudes investigated in this study, in terms of its correlation with peer status.

Consensual loving-rejecting was significantly correlated with twelve of the thirteen other variables in Table 21. The construct of loving-rejecting, regardless of the mode of measurement, was markedly related to measures of personality and acceptance-rejection of the child. Parents' self-reports on loving-rejecting evidenced slightly lower correlations, probably as a result of the bias of selecting socially desirable responses (Cox, 1966).

Intergroup comparisons of means on five measures of *casual-demanding* showed that mothers, but not fathers, tended to choose the more socially desirable response on scales of demanding and punishing (Cox, 1966). With the exception of mothers' self-report on casual-demanding, the several measures of this dimension conform to the hypothesis that casual parental attitudes are associated with higher social level; absence of tension in the family; healthy, self-satisfied, and outgoing children; and peer acceptance.

Analysis of the measures used for *overt concern* indicated a marked lack of agreement between ratings made by parents and by children, with parental responses biased in the direction of social desirability on the protecting and rewarding scales. The intercorrelations of the scores show a lack of relation between a child's ratings of a parent and a parent's self-ratings.

Characteristics of the Child. A basic assumption of the theoretical formulations in this study was that peer acceptance-rejection is strongly dependent on the stimulus value of the child in his peer society. The variables included as measures of child characteristics were assumed to represent major aspects of the individual to which peers respond. The results give strong support to that expectation. The child's personality and peer acceptance-rejection status were also expected and found to be related to parental attitudes and child-rearing practices and to family background factors.

Intelligence is generally conceptualized as ability to solve complex problems, including those of social, occupational, and economic adjustment. To a degree, social level reflects this intellectual capacity. It is not surprising, therefore, that the child's IQ is highly correlated with social level.

The moderate but significant pattern of correlations with parental child-rearing attitudes suggests that parents who are better educated and at higher social levels tend to have more intelligent children and to express more enlightened attitudes related to the rearing of their children than those at lower levels.

Theoretically, *self-concept* has roots in parental attitudes of loving-rejecting, and the child's perception of parental behaviors should be expected to be one of its correlates. The evidence supports the theoretical formulation to the extent that self-concept was significantly associated with the child's perception of each parent ($r = .56$, $p < .01$) as loving.

The association of *health problems* with parental loving-rejecting was significant. Low economic level and low parental education were family background factors correlated to poor physical health of the child.

Superego strength was measured in two ways. The two personality trait patterns obtained from teacher ratings had highly significant correlations with measures of family background and parental child-rearing attitudes. In general, the scores developed from the Class Play seemed to be suitable measures of the postulated behaviors. However, the four items selected for negative trait pattern A were among the least predictive of the 23 Class Play items available. On the other hand, the items selected as measures of negative trait pattern B were highly associated with the other variables.

Peer Acceptance-Rejection. Significant association with LM – LL was found for variables in each of the other sets.

FURTHER ANALYSES

Tables 21 and 22 present in detail the interrelationships among variables within and among family background, parental child-rearing practices and attitudes, personality and behavioral characteristics of the children, and the children's peer acceptance-rejection. The data in the following sections, taken from these two basic tables and from Cox (1966), emphasize some of the more interesting relationships between each variable and various measures of the other variables.

Correlations between Family Attitudes and Practices Dimensions and Choice Status. The correlations between the four scores on each of the three scales and the children's choice status scores are shown in the accompanying tabulation ($N = 97$ except for father's self-rating,

	Correlation
Loving-rejecting	
Child's rating of father	.54
Child's rating of mother	.38
Father's self-rating	.39
Mother's self-rating	.27
Casual-demanding	
Child's rating of father	.25
Child's rating of mother	.25
Father's self-rating	.27
Mother's self-rating	.17
Protecting (overt concern for child)	
Child's rating of father	.22
Child's rating of mother	.13
Father's self-rating	−.07
Mother's self-rating	−.06

where $N = 75$). The loving-rejecting scores correlate higher than the other two, and the correlation of peer status with the child's rating of his father's loving-rejecting behavior was higher than that with any other item. At the other end, the father's and mother's self-ratings on protecting (overt concern for the child) are not appreciably different from zero.

Parent Attitudes and Practices in Relation to Self-Concept, Medical History, IQ, and SES. The meaning of the parent attitude and behavior dimensions is further illuminated by a comparison with certain other variables. Table 23 shows the correlation of various scores of the three dimensions of the parental attitude and practices scale with the self-concept score, a medical history score, IQ, and parents' SES. As is indicated in the first column, the child's ratings of father and of mother on the loving-rejecting dimension correlate much higher with the self-concept score than do any of the other parental attitude and behavior scores. This indicates that the loving-rejecting scale, as completed by the child, functions to a considerable extent like a personality inventory, as does the self-concept scale. The mother's self-rating on loving-rejecting has a much lower correlation with the child's self-concept score.

Table 23. Child-Rearing Practices and Characteristics of the Child
(*N* = 97 Families)

Child-Rearing Practice	Self-Concept	Medical History	IQ	SES
Loving-rejecting				
Child's rating of father	.56	−.53	.42	.24
Child's rating of mother	.56	−.40	.41	.36
Mother's rating of self	.27	−.29	.21	.37
Casual-demanding				
Child's rating of father	.22	−.25	.08	.13
Child's rating of mother	.32	−.23	.08	.15
Mother's rating of self	.20	−.18	.14	.30
Protecting				
Child's rating of father	.17	−.12	.12	−.06
Child's rating of mother	.07	−.05	.12	.06
Mother's rating of self	−.09	.19	−.02	−.13

The child's rating of parents on loving-rejecting also correlates more highly than any other score with the medical history score. Children with higher IQ's felt more loved and less rejected than did those with lower intelligence. The mother's rating of herself on loving-rejecting correlates much less with IQ. The correlation of loving families, above average SES, higher IQ, and generally good child morale is not, of course, a new discovery. This is a multivariate cluster in which the good things in life tend to be correlated.

Self-Concept Scores versus Peer Status. Self-rating statements were obtained from pupils by two instruments, How I Feel About Myself (Piers & Harris, 1963) and the sra Junior Inventory, a problems checklist (Remmers & Bauernfeind, 1957).

The How I Feel About Myself instrument consisted of 80 statements to be answered yes or no, which could be scored in six subscales. Sample statements included: "My classmates make fun of me," "I am a happy person," and "I am smart." The correlations on this sample of the six self-concept subscales and a total self-concept score with peer status, are shown in the accompanying tabulation ($N = 97$). Here, as with the teacher ratings, the popularity scale correlated much more highly with peer status than any of the other scales. One result of this is that a total score combining all scales has a lower correlation with peer status than does the popularity scale alone.

	Correlations
Popularity	.62
Happiness	.44
Intelligence	.40
Appearance	.39
Behavior	.38
Anxiety	−.33
Total self-concept score	.50

An interesting light is thrown on the pupils' self-concept of popularity and their objectively determined peer status by comparing the popularity versus peer status correlation (.62) with the correlation between intelligence self-concept subscale and measured iq (.42). The child's recognition of his own intelligence level, as measured by this instrument, was less accurate than his awareness of his peer status. In fact, the intelligence self-concept scale correlated about as highly with peer status as it did with iq test scores.

Health Problems, Medical History. The health problems measure was based on information received from the mother during a home visit. Twenty-six items selected from the mother's report were included along with six items obtained from school records. The items used were adapted from related forms used in Cycle II of the U.S. National Health Survey. A history of many health problems also correlated with the child's scores on loving-rejecting (child's rating of father, −.53; child's rating of mother −.40) (see Table 21). The correlation of health problems with peer status was −.53. A history of poor physical health is adverse with respect to peer status.

Teacher Ratings on Various Characteristics. One approach to personality appraisal was the use of a 23-item set of teacher rating variables, adopted from Cattell (1963), for children's behavior traits. The items were bipolar; they were rated on a scale which contained 7 points from one extreme to the other. The correlations of those items which were most highly related to peer status scores are shown in the accompanying tabulation ($N = 97$). The seven items are ranked in order of their correlation with peer status.

	Correlation
Popular, generally liked by other children versus unpopular, generally disliked by other children	.75
Persevering, determined versus quitting, fickle	.57
Follows instructions easily and accurately versus has difficulty following instructions	.55
Neat, tidy, orderly versus untidy, careless with respect to appearance of self and belongings	.52
Adaptable, flexible versus rigid, has difficulty adjusting to changes or new situations	.50
Learns fast versus learns slowly	.49
Outgoing, mixes freely with other children versus shy, bashful, seclusive, aloof, remains fairly isolated from other children	.49

The first item, "popular-unpopular," correlates .75 with actual peer status. (For the sample including all the pupils involved in the main study [p. 67], the correlation obtained between TR and peer status was .57.) It may be noted that the "popular" item by itself correlated more highly with peer status than did composite scores made of any other combination of other items. The correlations with peer status of the rest of the items are not significantly different from one another.

Two of these, "has difficulty following instructions" and "learns slowly," are presumably related to IQ, which is in turn related to peer status. The remaining items contribute further information about liked-most and liked-least children as seen by their teachers.

The Class Play and Peer Acceptance-Rejection. The Class Play instrument, adapted from Bower (1960), is a modification of the guess-who procedure which has long been used as a means of obtaining peer nominations. The guess-who procedure gives a description of a kind of person and asks, "Who do you know that is like this?" In the Class Play technique the pupils are asked to suppose that the class is to put on a play and told to write in the name of the boy or girl who would most naturally fit 23 different parts. Sample items include: "Someone who gets angry at little things and gets into many fights," "A suspicious character who is not trusted by the others," "A person with a very bad temper." The nine items which yielded the highest correlations with peer acceptance-rejection are shown in the accompanying tabulation ($N = 97$).

Correlation

A suspicious character who is not trusted by the others .... −.62
A kind, considerate friend .... .55
Someone who is good natured and doesn't get angry over little things .... .55
A hermit who doesn't like to be with people .... −.53
Someone whom everyone likes and who tries to help everyone .... .52
A character who is a sloppy dresser — very careless about how he or she looks.. −.52
The laziest person in the world .... −.49
Someone to be class president .... .48
A neighbor who is careless with other people's property .... −.47

A composite score was computed for the five items shown with negative correlations. This correlated −.64 with peer acceptance-rejection as compared with the −.62 of the highest single item.

Some of the side correlations of this set of five items are of interest. They correlate negatively with IQ, with the "suspicious character" having the highest correlation (−.41). They tend to correlate more highly (negatively) with the total self-concept score than do any of the other items. They also tend to correlate positively with the health problems score, and more highly than the other items. The total picture of the child as seen by himself and by others tends to have considerable coherence.

Intercorrelations of Parental Attitude and Behavior Scales Scores. The various combinations of children's and parents' ratings scores yield some very interesting relationships. The first set compares the child's rating of mother with the child's rating of father on the three major scales for the 97 families (Table 24). It may be noted that these are both substantial in size and not significantly different from one another (.74, .71, and .72) on the three scales. Many children do not seem to discriminate much between treatment by mother and treatment by father. If a child rates his mother in a certain way, he also tends to rate his father similarly, on all three scales.

Table 24. Correlations of Roe-Siegelman Ratings of Parental Attitudes
and Behavior among Children, Fathers, and Mothers

Rating	Loving-Rejecting	Casual-Demanding	Protecting
Child's rating of mother vs. child's rating of father[a]	.74	.71	.72
Child's rating of mother vs. mother's self-rating[a]	.24	.33	.03
Child's rating of father vs. father's self-rating[b]	.31	.40	
Father's self-rating vs. mother's self-rating[b]	.32	.44	
Child's rating of father vs. mother's self-rating[b]	.29	.27	
Child's rating of mother vs. father's self-rating[b]	.21	.30	

[a]$N = 97$ families.   [b]$N = 75$ families.

The correlations between the child's rating of mother and mother's self-rating are much lower (.24, .33, .03) than the correlations between child's rating of mother and child's rating of father. In other words, a mother's behavior as seen by her child differs much more from her behavior as seen by herself than from the father's behavior as seen by the child.

The correlation for the first two dimensions between the child's rating of father and father's self-rating are quite similar to, and at least as high as, those for the child's rating of mother and mother's self-rating. The final comparison is that of the child's rating of father and mother's self-rating *with* the child's rating of mother and father's self-rating. These differ little. A comparison of the fifth and sixth items with the third and fourth items indicates that the ratings of the child toward one parent in comparison with the *other* parent's self-ratings are not appreciably different from the child's ratings of one parent and the *same* parent's self-rating.

Difference in Scale Response by Child and Mother for Different Scales. It is interesting to compare the correlations of the three major scale dimensions using the child's rating of father, child's rating of mother, and mother's self-ratings. These are shown in the accompanying tabulation ($N = 97$). The correlations between loving-rejecting and casual-demanding for the child's rating of father and child's rating of mother are almost identical. The correlation between these two scales

	Correlation
Loving-rejecting versus casual-demanding	
Child's rating of father	.39
Child's rating of mother	.40
Mother's self-rating	.27
Loving-rejecting versus protecting	
Child's rating of father	.41
Child's rating of mother	.32
Mother's self-rating	−.13
Casual-demanding versus protecting	
Child's rating of father	−.13
Child's rating of mother	−.10
Mother's self-rating	−.44

for the mother's self-ratings is slightly lower. The correlations between loving-rejecting and protecting (overt concern for the child) are similar in size to the first set for the child's rating of father and child's rating of mother. For the mother's self-ratings the correlation between loving-rejecting and protecting (overt concern for the child) becomes slightly negative.

From the child's point of view, loving is clearly positively related to expressions of overt concern, whereas the mother sees no relation between loving and overt concern for her child. For the third pairing of these scales, casual-demanding versus protecting (overt concern), the correlations for child's rating of father and child's rating of mother are slightly negative, but not much different from zero. The correlation between these two scales for mother's self-rating is .44. From the mother's point of view, demanding behavior is positively correlated with overt concern for her child; from the child's point of view there is essentially no relationship between demanding behavior and overt concern for him. There is clearly some difference in these two dimensions as seen by the children and the mothers.

SUMMARY

The relations of family background and parental attitudes in child rearing to the personality development and peer acceptance-rejection of the child constituted the problem of this study. A network of relationships among these four sets of variables was hypothesized, and strategically selected variables were employed to examine pivotal linkages. Significant relationships in support of the theoretical formulations were found throughout the hypothetical network. The significant linkages established here were interpreted as clarifying some of the major factors which influence personality development and peer acceptance-rejection. Although correlational evidence is inadequate by itself to support causal inferences, the sequential relations of the sets of variables examined and the developmental frame of reference involved are believed to justify the following conclusions.

FAMILY BACKGROUND

Social Level. This family background factor is associated with the degree of enlightenment displayed in child-rearing attitudes and practices, with the extent to which the child develops psychologically favorable attributes, and with the child's capacity for effective socialization which affects his acceptance or rejection by peers.

Adverse Family Factors. Factors contributing to the adverse family factors index are positively related to disruption and dissent in the family, with psychologically harmful and conflicting child-rearing attitudes and practices of parents, with hostile and negative child personality trait patterns, and with peer rejection.

PARENTAL CHILD-REARING PRACTICES AND ATTITUDES

Loving-Rejecting. In addition to linkages with family background factors, discussed above, the degree of love or rejection projected by parents seems to have marked influence on the cognitive, personality, and social development of the child.

Casual-Demanding. This dimension demonstrated statistically correlations with significant personality development and peer acceptance-rejection, but fewer significant linkages with factors in the family background were manifested than were for the loving-rejecting scale.

Overt Concern. The scales for overt concern used in this study appear to have measured something somewhat different as seen by parents and as seen by children. There was no area of agreement between scores based on parents' self-reports and scores based on the child's perception of that parent; the number of significant correlations with other variables in the network, although in the hypothesized direction, were only slightly better than chance expectancy.

Parental Consistency. These results confirm that disagreement between parents in child-rearing attitudes and practices has a substantial influence on the child's personality development. The highly significant associations of parental disagreement with measures of tension in the family and low social level are noteworthy.

CHARACTERISTICS OF THE CHILD

Intelligence. The highest correlation of IQ was that with social level; only a moderate association was found with parental child-rearing attitudes and practices.

Ego Development. This factor, measured by two instruments, was most significantly influenced by parental attitudes of loving-rejecting. Low self-concept was associated with parental rejection. An appreciable association was found between the child's self-concept, teacher ratings based on observed behaviors, and peer status.

Personality Traits. Personality trait patterns based on teacher ratings were almost equally related to family background measures and to measures of parental child-rearing attitudes and practices. Ratings of popularity were enough more highly related to peer status than other rating variables to indicate that likableness has a good deal of uniqueness, which is not accounted for by its correlations with other personality characteristics.

Of the two scores developed from the Class Play technique only one, Negative Trait Pattern B, correlated significantly with most of the variables in the matrix. On the other hand, the four items selected for Negative Trait Pattern A were among the least predictive of the 23 Class Play items.

Peer Acceptance-Rejection. The stimulus value of the child, reflected in personality traits, health, intelligence, and self-concept, seems to be the principal determiner of peer acceptance-rejection. Accepted children tend to be outgoing, friendly, healthy, and bright, whereas those rejected by peers tend to be hostile, antagonizing, in poor health, and mentally dull.

If we order the whole set of variables dealt with in this chapter in terms of their correlations with our main interest, peer acceptance-rejection status, the highest degree of relationship is shown with teacher ratings on popularity and with a combination of items from the Class Play. These are essentially alternate ways of obtaining information about peer status. At about the same level is the self-concept of one's own popularity, indicating a substantial accuracy on the part of children in estimating their own peer status.

At a somewhat lower level of relationship with acceptance-rejection are those variables covering subjective expressions of attitude by the children (the problem checklist and the self-concept scales) and more nearly objective factors (the medical history of the child, a list of adverse family factors, and the child's IQ). On the parental attitude and behavior scale, the child's responses concerning his parents' attitudes and behavior on the loving-rejecting scale were related to peer acceptance-rejection at about the same level as were these latter variables. The self-rating by father and by mother on the parental attitude and behavior scales correlated lower with peer status than had been expected. Correlations with peer status were higher with the loving-rejecting scale than with the other two parental attitude scales.

8

~~~~~~

Peer Status and Juvenile Delinquency in Relation to Socioeconomic Status

Juvenile delinquency is one socially significant later behavior category which could be expected to be related to measures of peer acceptance-rejection. Other real-life categories of this kind include dropping out of school, treatment in a child guidance clinic, and eventually the presence of adult maladjustments of various kinds. Roff (1961b, 1963b, 1964, 1969) has shown that a record of delinquency is predictive of adult criminal behavior in only a minority of cases. However, the problem of the prediction of delinquency remains an important one from both a theoretical and practical point of view.

Although the term *juvenile delinquency* sounds definite, its actual definition, and practices in dealing with it, vary from place to place and from time to time. One dictionary definition is "a transgression of law . . . or offense. Or: a tendency to commit such offenses." In practice, there are various degrees of juvenile delinquency, defined not only in terms of offenses but also in terms of the apprehension and treatment of the offender. First is breaking a minor law without being discovered; everyone has done this at one time or another. Another degree is being detected by a policeman and verbally corrected, perhaps remaining anonymous. This may occur with juveniles, as it may occur with adults for minor traffic offenses; it is impossible to get accurate information on the frequency of these incidents. A degree above this is apprehension and more formal admonition, either by an arresting officer or at a juvenile department. A great many youngsters have no further contact with the law after such an occurrence. Some, however, following further trouble or a more serious offense, are brought into juvenile court, where they may be adjudicated delinquent and put under supervision or on probation.

Because it has certain administrative definiteness, adjudication is the most commonly used single criterion of delinquency in studies in this area. Like many other seemingly clear-cut administrative actions, its definiteness as a criterion is more apparent than real, since the frequency with which youngsters are "adjudicated" varies from place to place, from judge to judge, and from probation office to probation office. In any case, many youngsters never reappear in juvenile court. If there is further trouble, a youngster may be taken out of an unsatisfactory home and neighborhood situation. In both the cities dealt with here, he could be sent to a county training school. It is easily possible to get a count of these individuals; other work with Minnesota groups by Roff (1964) indicates that about one out of five boys from the county training school committed subsequent offenses and were sent to the state training school. Later, a higher proportion of those sent to the state training school appear as adult offenders than of those sent only to the county training schools. A small number of these, who represent by this time a *very* small percentage of the total population, are sent to a penitentiary.

PROCEDURE

Information concerning delinquency was obtained for the Minnesota cities during the summer of 1966. In the first city, this follow-up was four years after the initial peer status scores were obtained. In the second city, where testing started a year later, the interval was three years. Since all those for whom data were initially obtained were in the third through sixth grades, the oldest children in the first city would have completed only the tenth grade, and in the second, the ninth. Thus the results presented here are referred to as relating to "early" delinquency.

The term *delinquency* as used here includes all cases in each city who had contact with the juvenile authorities formal enough to result in the preparation of a case file. Most, but not all, of these were adjudicated delinquents. Almost all of their offenses occurred before the age of sixteen. One consequence of this is that the difference in total frequency between socioeconomic levels is not quite so sharp as it is if juvenile delinquents of all ages are counted. Even if subsequent work including juvenile delinquents of all ages should change the picture presented here, any validity that this study of early delinquents may have will not be affected. Further follow-up studies might simply lead to the recognition of a difference between early delinquency and later delinquency, which has received some, but very little, attention (Neumeyer, 1961).

Delinquency information was originally obtained only for boys in the first city for whom teacher interviews were available. A search of delinquency records was made during the summer of 1966 for such boys in all four grades. In the second city, a search was made for all fifth and sixth grade boys from the first year of testing, whether or not interviews were available. These boys were more likely to have a delinquency record than the third- and fourth-graders, and both time and funds were limited. Since delinquency is much more frequent among boys, a search for the comparable groups of girls was postponed.

Of the 800 boys in the first city for whom a search was made, delinquency files were found for 87, or approximately 11 per cent. A file meant that a boy had been apprehended, and had gotten beyond a preliminary consideration. The file presented the circumstances of his misbehavior and indicated the steps taken in an attempt to assist him. Allowing for the attrition in the sample owing to those who moved away from the city, the 87 found cases are definitely more than 11 per cent of those still present in the area. It should be remembered that these boys, who were in the sixth through tenth grades at the time of the follow-up, are far from being through the delinquency period.

The schools in each Minnesota city had already been divided into SES quartiles. In the first city, schools of all four socioeconomic quartiles were used. In the second, only schools from the third and fourth quartiles were used, representing the lower socioeconomic half of the city. The latter provided enough pupils to meet the preset sample size, and involved the areas with the greatest incidence of later problem behavior.

RESULTS

The first cases to be run through the delinquency records were the first city boys for whom interviews had been obtained. It was decided to start with these because (a) the four socioeconomic quartiles for the entire city were represented, (b) the interval since first testing was one year longer than in the second city, and (c) it would be helpful to have the additional information contained in the teacher interviews for all those with records of delinquency. It was found that the proportion of delinquents in the low peer status group consistently exceeded the number in the high and middle score groups in the three upper SES quartiles. This was in line with expectations. In the fourth SES quartile, however, the number of delinquents among the high-choice pupils was about as high as¯the number in the low-choice group. This was contrary to expectations and, taken by itself, might seem a chance effect.

A similar study was immediately run for the second city. In other parts of this project, it had been assumed that SES quartiles were a fine enough subdivision for most purposes. It was decided that it would be worthwhile to divide the two quartiles (only the lower two were available for this city) in half, to produce octiles (since there would have been eight of these if the entire sample of schools had been used). Since we had only the third and fourth SES quartiles of these schools, the resulting octiles are numbered 5 through 8, to indicate that they are from the lower half of the entire school population. This division was made by schools rather than by individual pupils, so the actual number of pupils in the population varies slightly from one octile to another.

These octiles were examined for delinquency frequencies in relation to choice scores. It was found that there were no delinquents at all among the high-choice or middle-choice boys in SES octiles 5 and 6, and only one in octile 7. There were a substantial number of low-choice boys with delinquency records. In octile 8, however, there were at least as many high-choice boys as low-choice boys with delinquency records, thus replicating the first city results almost exactly. Since there was an observable difference between octiles 7 and 8 in the second city, it was decided to return to the first city data to separate quartiles III and IV into octiles. Again, for octiles 5, 6, and 7, the results were in line with the original expectation that low-choice boys would show substantially more delinquency. For octile 8, on the other hand, delinquency was slightly more frequent among the high-choice boys than among the low-choice, in accordance with what was becoming the revised expectation.

To fill in the omissions resulting from the use of only boys for whom interviews were available, information concerning delinquency was next obtained in the second city for *all* the 1,729 fifth- and sixth-

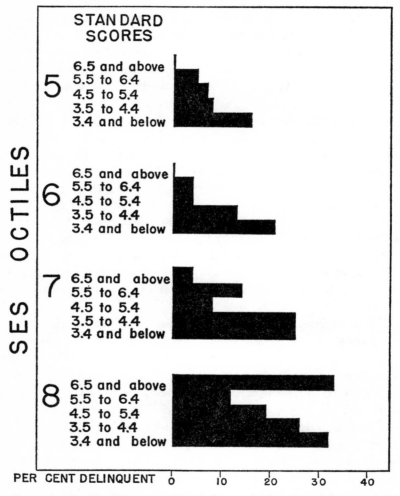

Figure 4. Juvenile delinquency in relation to earlier peer choice status at different socioeconomic levels. Reprinted by permission from M. Roff and S. B. Sells, "Juvenile Delinquency in Relation to Peer Acceptance-Rejection and Socioeconomic Status," *Psychology in the Schools*, 1968, 5, 3–18.

grade boys for whom first-year peer scores had been obtained. The total number found in the delinquency files was 187, or 11 per cent. Figure 4 shows the percentage delinquent for five standard peer score class intervals of choice status, for the four octiles of the schools in the lower SES half of the city. The exact numerical values are given in Table 25. Again, the original expectations were approximated closely except for the boys with standard scores of 6.5 and above in octile 8. Here, the proportion delinquent was almost exactly the same as that for the low-choice group with standard scores of 3.4 and below. The

Table 25. Juvenile Delinquency in Relation to Earlier Peer
Acceptance-Rejection, by SES ($N = 1,729$)

Choice Scores	Total N	N Delinquent	Percentage Delinquent
Octile 5			
6.5 and above	25	0	
5.5–6.4	113	6	5
4.5–5.4	191	14	7
3.5–4.4	73	6	8
3.4 and below	30	5	16
Total	432	31	7
Octile 6			
6.5 and above	24	0	
5.5–6.4	144	6	4
4.5–5.4	249	9	4
3.5–4.4	78	10	13
3.4 and below	42	9	21
Total	537	34	6
Octile 7			
6.5 and above	24	1	4
5.5–6.4	110	15	14
4.5–5.4	157	12	8
3.5–4.4	89	22	25
3.4 and below	24	6	25
Total	404	56	14
Octile 8			
6.5 and above	18	6	33
5.5–6.4	104	8	8
4.5–5.4	144	27	19
3.5–4.4	65	17	26
3.4 and below	25	8	32
Total	356	66	19

other standard scores for the eighth octile showed the same sort of pattern as the scores in the other octiles.

This effect — the high-choice boys showing at least as much delinquency as the low-choice boys in SES octile 8 only — appears in the large sample in the second city and in a smaller sample in the first city. (Results for the total sample in the first city have not yet been obtained.) This is superimposed on the finding of a decrease in amount of delinquency with an increase in peer acceptance-rejection scores at the other socioeconomic levels.

ILLUSTRATIVE CASES

The qualitative descriptions of children's behavior and life situations have been useful in many ways. In the present context, they give information not given by the peer acceptance-rejection score about the delinquent as seen by school personnel; they include various factors which may relate to his behavior, both at the time of the interview and later. Selected cases are presented here to illustrate high- and low-choice children, delinquent sooner or later, at different socioeconomic levels. (For more detailed and comprehensive case histories of children, with substantially more family information, see Roff, Mink, & Hinrichs, 1966.)

Upper SES. There was only one high-choice delinquent in the upper SES quartile from the interview group. Thus, the first illustrations of the behavior characteristics of high- and low-choice youngsters are this high-choice boy (Frank) and two low-choice boys from high SES schools (Thomas and John).

❦❦❦❦❦

Frank (sixth grade) is a large, fat boy, extremely shy, who always looks dirty and unkempt, his clothes messy and his hair uncombed. Although he can do things all right, he looks awkward when doing them, particularly writing. He never volunteers for anything. He has been absent a great deal, usually three or four days at a time, with stomach trouble due to extreme nervousness. He is good at his work, tries hard, and when absent always makes an effort to do the makeup work so that he can keep up with the class. He is self-effacing, seems quite embarrassed when called on and shows much ambivalence about volunteering. On the other hand, he is beginning to take part in teenage activity; they giggle and laugh about the other sex. He is quite upset when reprimanded. The teacher feels that in some ways this activity is an improvement, and she would rather put up with much of his play with the other kids as long as he is doing what seems more natural and normal for him. She has had him for two years and has seen a decided change in his behavior, particularly in asserting himself more than he used to do.

On the whole, though, Frank is still a rather passive individual in class. On the playground, he is thoroughly active in the games. He speaks in a tiny voice and seems afraid to make mistakes. He gives the impression that he would die if he made another mistake. He does not demand much attention of the teacher, just accepts her.

The other boys accept him well; he talks to them easily. They choose him on their sides when there is some sort of contest, and they give him much recognition when he does something well.

Little information on the family except that his mother was divorced from his father and is now remarried. Frank reflects his stepfather's interest in him and talks about the stepfather's experiences. The mother is cooperative toward the school, and the teacher feels that Frank definitely reflects kindness from mother and stepfather.

Probation Information: Two years after testing, malicious destruction of property. Referred to parents. About a year later, mother became overtly psychotic. Soon after this, he was arrested for auto theft and placed on probation.

∞∞∞∞

Thomas is an average-size sixth grader with fairly good development. He possesses average physical skills and generally can hold his own on the playground. Teacher estimates that he has above average ability; however, achievement is not up to what might be expected. Rather poor general adjustment. He is quite a problem. Has to be watched carefully. Major misbehavior such as throwing stones at cars and lighting matches on the school stairs. He is untruthful and antagonistic, both toward teacher and classmates, so in general he is not well liked by his peers. He has one friend, a boy who is also known as a troublemaker.

Thomas is restless, constantly on the move. The teacher believes that he has good possibilities. He is able to reason in a fairly mature fashion and seems quite sensible when called upon to discuss life in general. Both parents are working, and the three boys are left alone a good deal of the time. The teacher knows the parents are in disagreement as to how to handle the disciplinary problems. His father has rather strict standards, but the mother is very permissive and perhaps unconcerned.

Probation Information: Age 16 — possession of liquor and drunk. No record of either social agency contact or contact with the law for any other member of the family.

~~~~~~

John (fifth grade) is a very large boy, the largest in the class. He is one year older than the others, having failed one year. Last year he broke his leg and he was somewhat lame; it is getting better now although he still is somewhat awkward at times.

He is a bully. He picks on younger children and does not play well with the kids in his classroom. He is one of the last chosen on the playground.

He is an apple polisher; he tries very hard to work his way into the group of most popular children.

In the classroom he is very good, quiet, cooperative, and causes no disturbance. You hardly know he is in the room. Academically, he is below average, has a very difficult time getting his schoolwork done, but he works at his assignments.

He is domineering toward other children. He takes it out on smaller classmates and singles them out one at a time for picking on. He teases them, holds them down, takes their hats away, etc. His aggressiveness is not confined to overt fighting but rather to some form of passive aggressiveness, holding a child down to say uncle and not letting him go, or teasing. Most of the students let him alone. The smaller ones dislike him intensely and fight him off. His relationship to the teacher is very good. He does what he is told and causes no trouble in the classroom. He tries to please the teacher and he brings things from home to show the teacher and the class. The trouble he is experiencing is all out of doors.

The stepmother is described as very good. She will go to bat for the children. When they are wrong, she will punish them. John is the second youngest of five children, four of them boys. At home there is a rather rough and tumble life, and John is picked on, being somewhat duller than his siblings.

Probation Information: At age 15, burglary. Lives with father and stepmother. There is no history of contact with any social agency, nor of any contact with the law by any other member of his family.

~~~~~~

Middle SES. Space does not permit the presentation of cases for all possible combinations of SES and choice status. Low-choice boys with subsequent delinquencies from SES quartiles II and III are presented next. For both of these SES groups, the number of high-choice boys who became delinquent is very small.

Paul is a very small, undernourished fourth-grader who has a cute face. He talks babytalk at times. He has no marked strengths. He is often dishonest at games, and he generally makes a poor adjustment with others. Nevertheless, the teacher pointed out, there is some indescribable quality that makes this youngster likable by adults.

On the playground, he is aggressive at times with other youngsters. He enters games and seems to enjoy them. In the classroom, he was described as sneaky, sometimes bad tempered. He treats others in the classroom in an aloof manner. He visits others occasionally but seems not to become too personally involved in social contacts. The group also treats him in an aloof, distant manner. The teacher can correct and guide this youngster when he is not behaving properly. He has never shown any strong feelings toward the teacher.

He is totally disliked. The girls dislike him and the boys dislike him. The girls dislike him because he beats them up, and the boys dislike him because he is sneaky and because he doesn't follow the group's standards of behavior. He disturbs them because he does not follow directions and he is not fair.

The family is large and somewhat lower economically than their neighbors. The parents are not effective in directing Paul or his siblings. There are economic problems that the family must face. The mother does not follow through consistently on any plan concerning the youngsters.

Probation Information: When in second grade, he was picked up on three separate occasions within one week: once for burglary, twice for petty larceny. No charge was placed. The following summer, he was arrested for burglary and put on probation for two years. Soon after school started, again caught for petty larceny. In the spring when in the third grade, he was arrested for burglary and sent to county training school. On release, again charged with burglary and prowling cars. Two months after peer rating, burglary and arson, and again sent to detention home.

The father has a history of five arrests for assault and battery, drunkenness, and wife-beating. About a year after testing, father hospitalized as psychotic. Oldest brother had history of six arrests, next brother had one arrest, oldest sister had six arrests, next brother had three arrests, and next sister had seven arrests. Mother described as showing serious emotional disturbance.

Probation report while in second grade: quite perceptive and capable of independent thinking and expressing himself. Open negative feeling to father. Lives for present. Expect severe destructive aggression in future. Severe character disorder manifested by impulsive acting out, impaired ability to enter into meaningful relations with others and considerable immature narcissism.

Mother and father divorced when Paul was in sixth grade; they tried to give him some attention but this was difficult with ten children. Both drank too much.

≈≈≈≈≈≈

Randy (sixth grade) is a small, wiry boy with flashing eyes, a big smile and usually neat appearance. Devil-may-care attitude. He doesn't seem to care if school keeps or not. Highly self-seeking, self-pushing, egocentric. Seems to need to make sure that everyone knows he is intelligent. He is very verbal, loves to recite orally, but hates written work. Tremendous memory for facts which he acquires from reading, TV, and radio. He is a complete individualist. He isn't at all like the other children except that he does seem to want their approval. His answer to a list of offenses told him by the teacher was in the nature of debating style. "Now in the first place, I did not . . ." and so forth. He counts them off on his fingers. His strengths are his quick mind and wit, and his ability to think something through, although an IQ test suggests his ability is less than teacher had supposed. He is almost analytical in his thinking. He has the ability to bluff. His greatest weakness is his complete lack of motivation. He seems willing to be far less than the best academically, partly because he is unwilling to reveal his short-comings. He is almost criminal-like in his tendency to shift blame. Two juvenile officers came to school to talk to him about vandalism in a closed store, and with an innocent look he sent them to the junior high school to talk with his older brother, who was really just an onlooker. The officers soon returned.

On the playground, he wants to be a big leader, a strategist. He would have been a good Nazi. He is not outright cruel to others, but he lacks understanding of their feelings and fears. No one else matters. He is a good competitor in class games, is not a poor loser, and is satisfactory in supervised play, but in unsupervised activity he wants to be the supreme dictator.

In the classroom his behavior is not exceptionally bad. He has a tendency to be polite when he is criticized, and he seems to take it well even though he gives excuses. He gets his name on the board for little things, and he is constantly reported by guides and patrols.

He has fairly normal relations with his peers, in spite of his acting so superior, for he doesn't act superior with all the boys, nor all the time. He irritates the girls because he acts so smart, and frequently interrupts. He wants to be very friendly with the teachers, but he has difficulty achieving this, for he feels that rules made for others don't apply to him. Rules are for the ignorant ones. He doesn't outright defy the teacher, rather he seems to ignore. Sometimes he grins as though he has to go along because it is necessary for the rest, but he seems to say that you know and I know that I really don't need these rules.

Most of the children pass Randy off. They have been used to him a long time. His cuteness and sharpness can't help but impress some of these kids, even though he irritates them. His patronizing attitude of cutting in on others' recitations is one of the reasons why the children react to him as they do. He is also too aggressive and is really a bully, even though he is small. He will even try his bullying on a larger child, but one who doesn't want to fight.

The parents are impressed by his factual knowledge, and they and his older brother and sister think he is cute. They are not as sharp as Randy. He is so well accepted by his family that he surely feels secure. A definite weakness is that the parents are not realistic in their appraisal, and they do not think the school appreciates their boy. They don't realize that he does not do the writing work expected of him, even though they have been told many times.

Probation Information: During spring of sixth grade, he was arrested for malicious destruction of property. There is no subsequent record.

❧❧❧❧

SES Octile 8. The SES level of greatest interest here is octile 8, in which there are as many high- as low-choice delinquents. The interviews indicate that in general the high-choice boys were in tune not only with the other boys, but also with the teacher and the school. Judging by their peer status and the interview data, they do not seem to be personality problems. On the other hand, the low-choice boys at this SES level are characteristically disliked by the other boys and more likely to be at odds with the teacher and the school. There has been a good deal of talk in the literature about the "delinquent subculture."

As a general explanation of all delinquency at this age level, this concept is clearly inadequate. It is closer to the facts to describe these delinquent boys as coming from a bottom economic level which produces more than its share of delinquents, whether as members of a delinquent subculture or through the operation of other factors, such as family disorganization, "improper" rearing, and so forth. Edward is a typical high-choice delinquent from the lowest SES group.

Edward (fifth grade) sometimes looks very neat and clean, and other times looks like he climbed out of a ragbag. Occasionally he doesn't even make it to school, apparently because of insufficient clothing. Edward is slender and appears undernourished. He is an attractive boy with a lot of drive. He probably is a good deal more sophisticated in the ways of the world than one would guess from his conversation. He's very nice and polite in school. Edward is a good student, but one handicap is that he rushes to get done.

Edward is a good ballplayer and a good sport and well liked and one of the first to be chosen on any athletic team. In class the youngsters also like him very well and are quick to choose him. He's usually mannerly. He's no bother to anyone, would quickly reach out to help others. He's dependable and is the best-liked boy in class. Good average intelligence. The teacher said that he could not be nicer to her; he's cooperative and courteous, wants to do well. He does things well, is quiet, does not make himself a pest. He does not ask for her help. I think part of this comes from his being forced to be independent of his disadvantaged family.

A very unfortunate home situation. Mother apparently does try to help work with the youngsters. Neither mother nor father attends conferences.

The father and mother could perhaps be adequate parents if they had one or two children, but with the extremely large family they have, they are both overwhelmed. As a result the youngsters do not get the proper care and emotional help that they should get. Father is frequently away from home, separated from the mother; mother, in seeking companionship, is apt to reach out to other men and to entertain them in her own home. This probably has some adverse effects for the youngsters. Both parents seem rather immature adults who are apt to satisfy their own needs before satisfying the needs of the youngsters. As a result, the children are many times left without the proper parental attention. Surprisingly enough, they seem to do quite well under these conditions. They are attractive, lovable, and likable boys and girls.

While there has been some petty thievery, some truancy, and some
lack of application on the part of these youngsters, by and large
they are happy, fairly well-organized boys and girls, who seemingly
make the most of what little life has offered them. Currently, there
has been talk by the welfare agencies of the possibility of removal
of the youngsters from this family. At this point, because of the
good adjustment made under these adverse circumstances, they have
been reluctant to move the older youngsters; it's the smaller ones
that would have the best chance to move on and more fully develop
their capacities, with the chance to live somewhere else.

Probation Information: Edward had been arrested for malicious
destruction of property and referred to his parents about a year
before testing. About a year and a half after testing, he was arrested
for shoplifting and put on probation for a year. Six months after
this probation, he was arrested for burglary; at that time he admitted nine other burglaries. He was sent to the county training
school, where he stayed for six months and remained on probation
for another six months after that. This brings him almost to the
time of the follow-up.

The family was well known to various social agencies. An older
brother was in an adult reformatory, and a second older brother was
on probation at the time of the follow-up. The family was described
as being unstable without the father. The mother seemed unable
to supervise. She had had an illegitimate child about two years
before follow-up. The psychological interview report said that there
was nothing grossly abnormal or unusual about Edward. Stable
mood, emotional reactions generally appropriate, though well
guarded; slightly unhappy, has a somewhat poor opinion about
himself, is fairly energetic — likes people. A normal person is
indicated.

Although this family situation seems definitely adverse, apparently Edward gets along surprisingly well. Of course, there has been
some petty thievery, truancy, etc., but both at the time of the initial
teacher interview and at the time of the probation interview,
Edward was judged to be a "normal person" who was exhibiting
some misbehavior.

~~~~~

A somewhat similar picture is given by Joe, also a high-choice boy
from the bottom SES group.

Joe (fifth grade) is small, short, and stocky, very handsome,
with a sparkling eye and a bright alert-looking face. He's very well

coordinated. Distinguishing him from other children are his quick smile, his sense of humor, and his tolerance and acceptance of others. He's extremely fair in all his dealings, seems to expect fairness in return and has a good healthy outlook on life. Has leadership ability, accepts responsibility well, has an inquisitive mind, and is rather adult-like in conversation.

Joe does very well in playground participation, respects the rights of others, and is a very good group member. He is looked up to for his athletic ability. He's often chosen as captain of a team, but this seems to be more because of his fairness in dealing with the other youngsters in a heated discussion than because of his athletic ability.

In the classroom he is very responsive. He participates willingly, volunteers regularly, has a great deal of background information. His tests indicate that he is overachieving. Youngsters are anxious to have him on committees and often look to him for leadership in class as well as on the playground and in the halls. He has been a good police boy. He's very well liked by the children. He has an older brother who has been involved in a great deal of delinquent behavior. The children have mentioned this to Joe, and he laughs and says, "Sometimes we are not all alike." He responds well to the teacher; he wants to please, but not in an anxious way. Joe accepts the teacher's role as a disciplinarian.

He comes from a disorganized family. His mother has been married three times. The whereabouts of his own father are unknown. He did not get along with his first stepfather but does relatively well with this one. He has one brother and several half-siblings. The mother and the current stepfather have been fairly cooperative with the school, coming for conferences. The mother feels that the youngsters are capable of caring for themselves and has given them an undue amount of freedom. Joe has been able to use this very well, while other members of the family have not. He is responsive to adults, respects authority, and generally is a happy, well-dispositioned child.

Probation Information: About 18 months before the study, when he was nine years old, he was arrested for petty larceny and referred to his parents. Two and a half years after testing, he was arrested for malicious destruction of property and referred to the school authorities. A year after that he was arrested for incorrigibility, truancy, and running away from home; placed on probation.

His older brother was sentenced to the penitentiary for several years, a few months before the time when Joe was tested.

〜〜〜〜〜〜

It may be noted that Joe's personality characteristics as described are generally very favorable ones. Neither originally nor later was he considered a personality problem. On the other hand, if we look at a pair of low-choice boys in this bottom SES group, we find not only reports of delinquency but also indications of personality difficulties. Jackie and James both illustrate this.

Jackie (fifth grade) is of average height, has fair hair, is fairly neat and clean — it varies. He is very loud, has a very mouthy, negative attitude. He can be caught right in the middle of doing something, and he will deny that he had anything to do with it. He takes pins out of the bulletin boards, pulls the shades, throws the flowers on the floor, pulls the bristles out of brooms. He usually thinks he is being very funny and has six or seven children egging him on. The teacher felt that he is entirely different from everyone in her room. He never works in the classroom. He does no spelling, no arithmetic, no reading. The teacher doesn't have too much trouble with him, but she is very dissatisfied with him. He is usually sent out of the room.
In the gym he is very uncooperative, not much coordination. He has to be protected to see that he gets his turn. He is not chosen very often; he doesn't play fair. If there is something that goes wrong he always blames somebody else.
The students do not like him because he creates problems. They think he is funny and they laugh, although he has no real friends. His relationship with the teacher is not good. He is very difficult to handle. The students laugh at him and encourage him to go on with this behavior, but basically he is left out of the group.
The family background is not very good. He is the second of six children. The mother has been caught for shoplifting, and there supposedly was a boyfriend with her. The father has a job once in a while. Most of the time he is working on his car. There seem to be many family problems; they have been encouraged to go to a family and children's service to get aid. Jackie's brother was sent through child study for a complete personality checkup and testing; they found that he needed status and this sort of thing. Jackie is showing somewhat the same behavior. He did go to remedial reading last year because of his inability to read, but he was absent so many times that he was not taken back this year. He is being seen by a special teacher on the average of two hours a day to help him gain some status by catching up academically.

Probation Information: Truancy and incorrigibility about a year after testing. Committed to the county training school for three months. Three months after that, violation of probation (truancy, absenting from home) — committed to county training school for an indefinite period. Within a week he ran away from training school again and was returned. Considered incorrigible and sent to state training school.

❧❧❧❧❧

James (sixth grade) is the youngest of three brothers. He is overweight and self-conscious about it. The children tease him. He is lazy, slow moving, frequently avoids physical effort.

His academic ability is better than his production indicates. It is difficult for him to get to work; but once he starts, he will stay at it. In fact, on occasion he has spent the entire day on arithmetic. He likes questions that require thinking.

James will hit back, kick, or swat anybody who walks past his desk. At times when in difficulty, he looks to the teacher for protection.

On the playground his sportsmanship is better than most of his teammates. His coordination is poor, but he likes to play. His coordination has improved somewhat this year.

In his classroom behavior, he aggressively acts out against the children and against the teacher. Teacher holds him briefly, in his more explosive moments. After he quiets down, he will go to work. Limits have to be set and firmly held for him.

He tries to buy friends through giving candy, gum, and so on. When he does not strike out against the children, some are apt to get him to do so. The children seem to have cast him in a role that will be very difficult for him to change. At the beginning of the school year, he screamed, lashed out at, or walked out on the teacher. Now he still gets angry and will try to fight the teacher, but he recovers from it more quickly and settles down more easily. There has been a slow but fairly consistent growth in self-control.

Children reject him. He almost demands this, despite his wanting to be liked and trying to buy friends. He starts many fights with children over petty things. The children fight back. He is gradually withdrawing from this kind of fighting, but if children really start a fight with him, he will fight it through.

The teacher has only talked with his mother by telephone. She is interested in James, overprotects him, and will take his side against any other information that might be offered.

Probation Information: In seventh grade, insubordinate in school; sent to county training school for six months.

Family had eight social agency contacts. Father attempted to murder mother and committed suicide when James was four years old. Mother is unstable, but willing to help. Psychological interview found: Impulsive, aggressive, seeks attention, many somatic complaints, inner self-control lacking. Marked dependency needs, poor peer relations, unresolved emotional conflicts (parents not desirous of seeking help) — not sociable.

High-choice Joe was mentioned for his fairness, whereas low-choice Jackie was described as "doesn't play fair." High-choice Edward was described as "very nice and polite in school," whereas low-choice James was described as "hitting anybody who walks past his desk." These pairs of boys seem to be at the extremes of more continua than that of peer status.

❧❧❧❧❧

Black Delinquents. Since there is a tendency in some areas for low economic status to be associated with race, it was a matter of concern to see to what extent, if at all, the phenomenon being discussed here was attributable to race. It was found that delinquent youngsters with both good and poor peer adjustment occurred in the black group as well as among white children. In these cities, less than 4 per cent of the entire grade school population were black, and many of their families were definitely above the lowest socioeconomic levels. The pattern found here may not fit other cities, such as New York or Chicago, where the population of black pupils is much larger, but it should fit a large number of cities where the ethnic composition does not differ too markedly from that of these cities.

Of the two cases presented here, Willy is not only liked by the other boys but he is also diligent in his schoolwork, although his ability level is not high.

Willy is a sixth-grade black boy, well coordinated and in good physical condition. He is the number two boy in the school in control. The boys respect him and a great many are afraid of him. He seems to be a leader. A consistent good sport on the playground. At times he protects the underdog, but on occasion he may kick him.

Willy is a very dependable monitor. In school he works hard. He is of dull normal ability. Even though he is slow in classwork, he does not want his assignments cut down for him. His effort is great enough to complete his work. He is not always right, but he certainly tries.

The teacher (a man) gives Willy responsibility in the classroom, and he carries it out consistently. He does not assume responsibility if it is not given to him. Boys respect and like him. There are several boys who would like to take his crown as number two man away from him. He is respectful, cooperative, and responsible. He is recognized by his peers for his leadership qualities. Strangely enough, for the position he holds in the estimation of the boys, he is not an aggressive leader. He always holds his own and gives an excellent account of himself when challenged. He rarely seems to challenge others.

There seems to be a gradual, consistent maturing in Willy this year. Children like his persistent trying, no matter what the job assigned.

His mother is cooperative with the school. She is much interested in her son. She wants him to be a good student and a good boy. Willy respects her and, on occasion, has told teacher of little things he has bought for his mother. They are a close family.

Probation Information: Two months after testing, charged with immoral conduct and placed on informal probation. One month after that, auto theft and sent to county training school. In spring of seventh grade, truancy and returned to county training school. The following summer, shoplifting. No further trouble until ninth grade when charged with driving without a license and disorderly conduct; informal probation.

Has five older and two younger siblings; two older brothers have histories of delinquency. Father is delivery man, mother is housewife. Probation interview notes "lacks strong male influence — quite close-knit family — good sibling relationship."

〰〰〰〰

On the other hand, Don is actively disliked and consistently non-conforming in the classroom. He has twelve siblings, some of whom also have records of delinquency. He is described as a boy who is not getting along well within his own peer culture.

Don (fifth grade) is a dirty, sloppy, well-built, apparently healthy, black boy. He is a nonconformist with little consideration of others or of the situation. Athletics is Don's only visible asset. His weaknesses are that he presents no apparent reasoning ability, is greatly retarded academically, and is very inconsiderate of others.

On the playground Don tries to run the show, tends to bully, is quick with the fists. He has good athletic ability and skills, but shows poor sportsmanship.

In the classroom he talks constantly. He is consistently non-conforming. Rules are made for everybody but him. With others he is inconsiderate of their feelings; he may even knock heads together. He delights in proving his physical strength, even in adverse ways. He is not interested in others except in order to show his strength.

With the teacher there is no communication either way. He may not answer at all; he often says "I don't know" and there continues to be an impasse, no outright conflict, but no real rapport possible. There has been no change in Don's behavior during the year.

Some children fear him because of his size, some are disgusted with his behavior and lack of cleanliness. He tends to intimidate those who fear him. His tangles with the law tend to appeal to some. Others may look to his ability in athletic skills. But even with the variety of responses, actual relationship with others is limited.

Don comes from a very large family. There are twelve or thirteen children; he is about in the middle. To observers there may appear to be parental apathy. However, there may be interests which are overlooked because of the overwhelming responsibility heaped upon this family. There is a sweet compliance on the part of the parents, but an inability to follow through with guidance and real care. The father remains employed, which is a decided family strength, but his livelihood is inconsistent. Actual physical surroundings are bare and sparse. There is sometimes not enough food and insufficient clothing. Some of Don's siblings are retarded, and several are in a great deal of trouble with the law.

Probation Information: First delinquency recorded while in third grade, breaking and entering and petty larceny. In two days during fourth grade, charged with four offenses, primarily shoplifting and petty larceny; placed on probation for a year. In fifth grade, insubordinate in school and probation extended. In May of fifth-grade year, bicycle theft, insubordinate in school; committed to county training school for an indefinite period. In fall of sixth grade, assault; probation continued. In spring of sixth grade, insubordinate in school; committed to state training school. Two older brothers and an older sister had records of repeated delinquency.

DISCUSSION

The contrast is sharp between the high- and low-choice boys in octile 8. The interviews presented above give a clear picture of the behavior of the low-choice delinquent boys as seen in school; they were obviously not well accepted by their peers. The high-choice boys got along well, not only with their peers, but also with the school. The teachers were not, of course, totally unaware of the peer status of the boys that they were describing. They had an opportunity to see the choices in the course of data collection, a month or two before the interview. More important than this, they were able to observe the children daily, and interviews concerning both boys and girls are full of comments such as "he (or she) is always the last to be chosen," or, "he (or she) is a leader and is usually the first one chosen on the playground (or in the classroom)." Choosing is a frequent activity, and youngsters who are not chosen can hardly fail to be aware that they are not.

Except for the bottom SES level, delinquency is progressively less frequent as choice scores rise. In the bottom SES group, this is also true except for the highest-choice boys. From earlier work, we would still expect these high-choice boys of the bottom SES group to make better adult adjustments than the low-choice boys.

This follow-up may be too early to reveal the kind of gang activity which is emphasized in some discussions of delinquency (Cohen, 1955; Short & Strodtbeck, 1965), and a later study of the group may give a somewhat different picture. On the other hand, a careful examination of discussions of gangs and delinquency indicates that they are frequently gang (rather than delinquency) oriented, and are not necessarily similar at all to the large number of cases of individual delinquency. With this reservation, it is of interest to compare the present findings with currently prominent viewpoints on delinquency. The literature on delinquency is extensive, and space does not permit a comprehensive review of it here. To place our findings in the context of one particular part of the literature, reference can be made to a conference report from the Children's Bureau, "Sociological Theories and Their Implications for Juvenile Delinquency" (Bordua, 1960). This gives a clear statement of two conflicting points of view, and will be quoted directly to avoid any appearance of caricaturing the position with which our results are in disagreement.

The two theoretical positions are frequently advanced to explain the occurrence of juvenile delinquency, including gang activity. One of these sees the delinquent subculture as

arising out of the socially structured gap between the aspirations of lower-class boys and the means realistically available to them to realize these aspirations. According to this view, lower-class socialization does not equip boys to perform according to the requirements of middle-class dominated institutions such as the school, and consequently the boys suffer "status deprivation" and low self-esteem. . . . The delinquent subculture values precisely what middle-class institutions devalue; e.g., "hanging around" instead of industriousness, aggressiveness instead of self-control.

"Status deprivation," then, provides the motivational core for the lower-class male delinquent subculture. . . . Equally crucial is the fact that "status punishment," in an institution such as the school, tends to be differentially concentrated in lower-class groups who are residentially concentrated in certain parts of any city [p. 3].

The second point of view sees the

beliefs and values of the street-corner group as arising, not from any situation of status deprivation, but as simply the adolescent version of "lower-class culture." . . . This position directly opposes the notion that the street gang or group's culture derives from a reaction to the demands of middle-class culture. Instead, it emphasizes the view that "lower-class culture," as a more or less systematized body of beliefs, values, "focal concerns" and even household forms, existed in its own right for generations and need not be considered as a reaction to beliefs, values, and household patterns of the middle-class [p. 4].

The present results clearly support the second point of view. They also offer clear-cut indications of differences in the patterns of delinquency at the upper and lowest social levels. At the upper social levels, delinquency appears as primarily a function of personality disturbance which is reflected by low peer status. Almost no high-choice boys from the upper levels were delinquent. At the bottom of the eight social levels, there was still a marked tendency for the low-choice boys to show delinquency more frequently than the middle boys, but the high-choice boys were delinquent as frequently as the low-choice boys. Qualitative information for high-choice delinquent boys at the fifth- and sixth-grade levels indicates quite clearly that they were not at that time in rebellion against that so-called middle-class institution, the school. They got along well with their associates and exhibited a reasonable amount of ambition scholastically. In some cases a boy had already shown some delinquency at the time of our study, and the teacher sometimes mentioned this as casually as she would the color of his hair. Most of these high-choice boys gave a clear picture at this age of being in tune with their associates, with the school, and with the teacher, although they sometimes came from highly pathological family situations.

It seems clear, and is replicated from one to the other of the two cities, that the lowest of the eight SES levels produces a substantial number of preadolescent boys who are not in any sense in general rebellion, although they may exhibit some delinquency, then and later. On the other hand, there is also a sizable group at the lowest social level which is similar to that found at higher levels, where delinquency is accompanied by low peer status, a more general personality disturbance, and a rebelliousness which clearly seems to be personally rather than class oriented.

This difference in pattern at different socioeconomic levels suggests a two-factor explanation of juvenile delinquency among boys: the personality factor, as reflected by peer status, operates almost alone at the upper and middle SES levels, whereas sometimes this personality factor and sometimes a cultural, and not the personality factor seems to be the primary influence in the lower SES group. The qualitative descriptions presented above illustrate concretely the action of these two factors.

Because of their natural preoccupation with cultures and subcultures, sociologists have tended to emphasize gangs and organized group activity in their discussions of delinquency. Although adolescent gang activity (recognized by some writers as occurring either in conjunction with, or independent of, delinquency) is common, it is unduly restrictive to limit discussion of delinquency to gang activity. Psychological or psychiatric discussions focus more on the characteristics of individuals that are associated with delinquency, whether the delinquency is on a group or individual basis. Again, there is a large literature which cannot be reviewed here in any detail. Mention must be made, however, of Jenkins' distinction between the socialized and unsocialized delinquent (1949).

Studies of delinquency employing the Minnesota Multiphasic Personality Inventory (Hathaway & Monachesi, 1953; Wirt & Briggs, 1959) contribute important information about differences in personality patterns between delinquents and non-delinquents but do not relate this in detail to socioeconomic status. Kvaraceus and Miller (1959), who have worked intensively with delinquents, have discussed some of the satisfactions which delinquent behavior can bring to adolescent boys, particularly in the lower class. Conger and Miller (1966), using a sample of tenth-grade pupils in an entire city, studied certain personality variables in relation to social class and delinquency. With a criterion of percentage of dilapidated homes in an area, they used a dichotomous division for social class which would not have revealed the differences found in the present study, even if they had been there. None of the factual information from any of these sources is incompatible with the results presented here, but none of these have combined the characteristics of individuals with a detailed breakdown by SES.

The criterion of delinquency used here was behavior serious enough to lead to a preparation of a delinquency file for a boy. This definition was adopted in earlier work on the later outcomes of delinquents because it seemed highly desirable to start with a definition broad enough to include all relevant cases. Occasionally, someone argues that *delinquency* is so vague a term as to be of no particular use in the behavioral sciences. As defined for the present study, it proved to be precise enough to give very meaningful relationships with the peer group phenomena we are studying.

9

∽∽∽∽∽

Summary

The primary aim of the work described in this book was the detailed analysis of the peer relations and peer status of children, including whatever concurrent correlations with other variables might be of interest and the longitudinal course of peer status and its relations to other socially important variables. Since some of these socially important variables might occur only infrequently, the basic research plan involved the use of a childhood sample large enough that we would have subsample sizes of some adequacy for follow-up studies. Another important feature of the research plan was the simultaneous study of schoolchildren drawn from two states, Minnesota and Texas, in different parts of the country, so that an immediate replication from populations differing in some respects was available. This series of studies investigated in detail not only the characteristics of peer acceptance-rejection scores obtained from pupils' choices of classmates, but also their relations to family background factors, measures of intelligence, birth order, ethnic group membership, school grades, and various personality characteristics. Also included was a study of the resemblance in peer status between ordinary siblings and between twins.

PROCEDURE AND SAMPLES, WITH ILLUSTRATIVE CASES

Peer choices of Like Most (LM) and Like Least (LL) and Teacher Ratings (TR) of peer status were obtained in the first year for 34,366 third- through sixth-grade pupils, about evenly divided between nineteen cities in Texas and two cities in Minnesota. The peer choices were obtained only from pupils of the same sex, on the assumption that satisfactory same-sex peer group adjustment is the major source of concern at these grade levels. IBM Mark Sense cards were used in the administration so that the entire set of data could be run on the computer. The use of computerized procedures made it possible to handle this quantity of material in a way which could not otherwise have been done. In addition to the totally computerized quantitative information, a substantial amount of qualitative information about high-, middle-, and low-choice pupils was obtained for assistance in interpreting the quantitative results.

Structured interviews with the teacher were carried out for a sample of low, middle, and high children from the total group studied. They contained information concerning the personal characteristics of the child, his behavior, the reaction of other pupils toward him, and his family situation.

Other available information which was regularly obtained both for cross-sectional analysis and for use in follow-up studies included IQ, birth order, socioeconomic level, and school achievement. Distributions of three main scores — Like Most, Like Least, and Like Most minus Like Least — are presented both graphically and tabularly. The combined LM – LL score is more nearly symmetrical in its distribution than either the LM or LL scores, whose distributions were somewhat asymmetrical.

Split-half reliability coefficients were obtained by correlating each child's choices by one-half of the same-sex members of the class with those of the other half. The coefficients so obtained are presented broken down by state, by grade, and by sex. No marked differences appeared consistently in relation to any of these three variables.

Although a great deal can be communicated by general concepts, descriptions of individual children are needed to give a comprehensive and meaningful picture of these children and their life situations. Condensed descriptions of children and their life situations, obtained through interviews, have been presented for boys and girls who vary in choice status and SES. These qualitative descriptions give concrete pictures of the differences in personality and life situation associated with choice status, sex, socioeconomic status, and school and family background. Other descriptions of this type are used from time to time in other places to supplement the quantitative scores.

INTERCORRELATIONS OF MEASURES, CROSS-SECTIONAL AND OVER TIME

Intercorrelations between the LM and LL scores were presented (.50 for the total sample), and the correlations of these and of the combination of the two of them with TR scores have also been presented for the entire first year elementary school sample for which complete scores were available ($N = 34,366$).

These were also presented separately for boys and girls, for the four school grades, for the two states, and for socioeconomic quartiles in one Minnesota city. There were no differences worthy of note by sex, by school grade, and by SES. The intercorrelations were slightly higher in Minnesota than in Texas. The correlations of peer scores with Teacher Ratings were essentially the same in all four SES quartiles. "Middle-class" teachers evaluated low-SES pupils just as accurately as they did middle- or high-SES children.

In Texas, where the average size of cities was smaller than in Minnesota, testing was continued through junior high school. As expected, owing in part to the change from spending all day with the same class in grade school to a shifting from class to class in junior high school, the intercorrelations, both cross-sectional and longitudinal, in the junior high school period were somewhat lower than those obtained in the lower grades.

Stability coefficients were given for peer status scores and TR's over one-, two-, and three-year intervals. In addition to the overall picture given of stability and change in these scores, comparisons have also been made of longitudinal trends by intervals between test administrations, by state, by sex, and by SES.

One-year stability coefficients were presented for peer choice scores and TR for grades three to four, four to five, and five to six for the total sample. The results showed no consistent trends of any kind in size of stability coefficients over a one-year interval at different grade levels.

Stability coefficients for the peer choice scores and TR for one-, two-, and three-year intervals were also presented. For the entire sample there was, as expected, a regular decrease with an increase in the test-retest interval. This decline was less marked in the LL and the TR scores than in the LM scores.

When boys are compared with girls, the LM stability correlations are consistently a little higher for girls than for boys for all three intervals. For the LL scores an initial difference in favor of the girls at a one-year interval vanished at the three-year interval. The stability coefficients for TR were consistently substantially higher for girls than for boys for all three intervals.

When Texas is compared with Minnesota, there are no consistent differences between states across the different intervals. The TR correlations were higher in Minnesota than in Texas over all three intervals. When the two lower SES quartiles are compared (Minnesota only), differences were small and unstable.

An intensive analysis has been presented of the correlations between Teacher Ratings of children and peer status scores. These can be regarded as indications of teacher accuracy in rating.

A teacher accuracy correlation of .57 was obtained for the entire first-year sample ($N = 34,366$). Little or no relationship was found between teacher accuracy and the following:

> elementary school grade
> sex of pupils
> Minnesota and Texas
> socioeconomic level

Another group of correlations was computed between the correlations of Teacher Ratings and peer status (LM – LL) for each teacher in the Minnesota sample who made ratings in both the first and second years of the study. These correlations indicate the amount of agreement or disagreement between the same teacher's accuracy in two successive years.

Little relationship was found between an individual teacher's accuracy one year and his or her accuracy the following year. Little relationship was found between an individual teacher's accuracy in rating the boys in his or her class and accuracy in rating the girls. The lack of substantial correlations between year-to-year accuracy and between accuracy for boys and accuracy for girls indicates that "teacher accuracy" cannot be considered an important characteristic of teachers. It was suggested that differences in teacher accuracy can be accounted for in part by differences in dispersion of peer acceptance scores from class to class.

PEER STATUS IN RELATION TO CHOOSER AND CHOSEN,
TWIN AND SIBLING RESEMBLANCES, IQ AND SES,
AND BIRTH ORDER

The correlation between the positive choice scores (LM) of choosers and chosen was .024 in Minnesota and .017 in Texas. For the LL scores the corresponding correlations were −.152 (Minnesota) and −.160 (Texas). Just as there was no appreciable difference in the correlations in the two states, so there was no appreciable difference in the chooser-chosen correlations, positive or negative, by school grade, by sex, or by socioeconomic levels.

The relation between these results and different kinds of studies of "social perception" was discussed.

Correlations have been presented between identical twins, fraternal twins, and non-twin siblings, broken down where appropriate by sex. Attention was focused primarily on the LM − LL score; results for other scores are presented in Appendix B. There was a consistent change in these correlations from identical twins to fraternal twins to siblings (.70, .52, and .31, respectively). For the combined peer-teacher score, these correlations rose to .77, .53, and .36. The correlations for fraternal twins and for non-twin siblings were somewhat higher for like-sex than for unlike-sex pairs. The resemblance in scores between different members of the same family was clearly established.

Scores on the Lorge-Thorndike Intelligence Test were available for all fourth-grade classes ($N = 2,800$) in the first Minnesota city. The schools were classified into quartiles on SES, making use of a combination of adult income and education from the 1960 census values. At each of these four SES levels, the group of high boys and high girls, defined as those with sociometric scores 1 SD or more above the mean, were compared in IQ with the low boys and low girls, defined as those with sociometric scores 1 SD or more below the mean. The difference between the high and low groups at different SES levels ranged from 11.5 to 22.1 IQ points with all but three values falling between 15 and 20 points. There was no consistent trend for the difference in IQ between high and low girls or boys to be greater at one SES level than another. The problem of social adjustment indicated here is not ordinarily recognized in discussions of the desirability of mixing children from all socioeconomic levels with the aim of equalizing educational opportunity.

A study was made of the relation between birth order and peer status for 2,957 children in Texas. The most favored position by a slight margin, from the point of view of peer status, was the second (younger) of two children. The next best was the youngest child of three or more. The least favorable situation was in the middle-of-four-or-more children. Here birth order is confounded with family size, which in turn has some negative correlation with SES. Although the differences described here are definite, they are not large. Our results for peer status are thus quite similar to the situation described many years ago by Harold Jones, who observed that "psychological differences within the various birth orders have, as a rule, been small in magnitude" (1933).

CHILDREN WITH SPANISH SURNAMES

Comparisons have been presented between a sample of children with Spanish surnames and a control group consisting of other pupils from the same classes. Because of the possibility of a difference in the peer status of these groups in the two states, separate results were presented for Texas and Minnesota. Separate comparisons have been made and these samples have been broken down in other ways, with the following results.

There is a slight but definite difference in favor of the control group on the LM scores in Texas, but not in Minnesota. For LL scores there is no significant difference between the Spanish surname and control groups in either state. When the scores were compared separately for boys and for girls, there is a slightly greater difference between the two groups for girls than for boys. This difference is too small to be of any practical significance.

For the Minnesota sample only, scores for the Spanish surname and control groups were compared at each of four grade levels (third through sixth). No trend in relation to grade level was apparent. Also, a comparison of the two groups was made for the four quartiles in socioeconomic status. No consistent trend appeared.

Point biserial correlations were computed to obtain a correlational expression of the group differences in peer scores. The highest of these was .16 for girls in Texas.

Qualitative descriptions of children differing in peer status, grade, sex, SES, and proportion of Spanish surname children in a school were presented.

PEER STATUS AND FAMILY BACKGROUND FACTORS

Analyses were made of the relation between peer status and family background factors, using three different sets of family information. The first of these was the structured interview information about children and their families which had been obtained in Minnesota. Frequencies of occurrence of different kinds of family characteristics were tabulated for pupils who were high, average, and low in peer status. Attention was also paid to SES. Positive factors included such things as family harmony and cohesiveness. Neutral factors included such things as mother's employment outside the home, and stepparents. Negative descriptions referred to unstable, tense, unhappy families. Infrequently mentioned factors which are possibly negative include such statements as child is spoiled and overindulged, parents are inconsistent, and parent is or has been imprisoned. Some of these were significantly related to SES and some were not.

A second approach made use of an open-end questionnaire for a sample of 685 Texas pupils, again comparing children of high and low peer status. The information obtained was oriented more toward negative than toward positive factors. Items which appeared related to peer status included a history of being on welfare, a criminal history, and a history of moving around with unusual frequency.

The third approach made use of a questionnaire for structured interviews concerning family background factors which was administered to a sample of 59 Texas families. The quantitative analysis of the results of these interviews agrees with the preceding study in suggesting a correspondence between degree of family pathology and peer rejection among the children involved. Scales for two factors, Family

Background Problems and Unfavorable Parental Attitudes, were scored. Both proved effective in discriminating between families of children of high and low peer status.

THE INTERRELATIONS OF FAMILY FACTORS, RATED PERSONALITY CHARACTERISTICS, SELF-CONCEPTS, AND PEER STATUS

Selected data from a doctoral thesis carried out in connection with the project by S. H. Cox (1966) are presented. Socioeconomic status, family background, parental child-rearing attitudes and practices, and characteristics of the child, as these relate to one another and to the child's peer status, were studied intensively on a subsample of approximately 100 families. Among the instruments used were the Roe-Siegelman scale of child-rearing attitudes and practices, a self-concept scale, How I Feel About Myself (Piers & Harris, 1963), teacher ratings on 5 bipolar traits (Cattell, 1963), and the Class Play procedure (Bower, 1960).

When the whole set of variables dealt with in Chapter 7 are ordered in terms of their correlations with measured peer status, the highest degree of relationship is shown with teacher ratings on popularity and with a combination of items from the Class Play. These are essentially alternate ways of obtaining information about peer status. At about the same level is the self-concept of one's own popularity, indicating a substantial accuracy on the part of children in estimating their own peer status.

At a somewhat lower level of relationship with acceptance-rejection are those variables covering subjective expressions of attitude by the children (the problem checklist and the self-concept scales) and more nearly objective factors (the medical history of the child, a list of adverse family factors, and the child's IQ). On the parental attitude and behavior scale, the child's responses concerning his parents' attitudes and behavior on the loving-rejecting scale were related to peer acceptance-rejection at about the same level as the more nearly objective family factors. The self-rating by father and by mother on the parental attitude and behavior scales correlated less with peer status than had been expected.

PEER STATUS IN RELATION TO JUVENILE DELINQUENCY
AT DIFFERENT SOCIOECONOMIC LEVELS

A follow-up study, in terms of records of juvenile delinquency, was made for samples in the two Minnesota cities. At the time of follow-up, the oldest boys had reached the tenth grade in one city and the ninth grade in the other. Since additional delinquency would be expected in these groups with increasing age, the delinquency discussed in this paper has been referred to as "early." In both Minnesota cities it was found that the relationship between earlier peer status and delinquency was not the same at different socioeconomic levels: at the upper and middle levels, delinquency tended to occur in boys who had been rejected by other boys, and there was almost no delinquency among the high-choice boys. At the lowest level, delinquency unexpectedly occurred with about equal frequency among the most-rejected and the best-liked boys.

There seems to be what may be called a two-factor explanation of delinquency. At the upper and middle socioeconomic levels, delinquents tend to be those with personality difficulties, as reflected in rejection by other boys. At the lowest socioeconomic levels, delinquency seems attributable in part to personality difficulty (as reflected by poor peer status) and in part to a direct expression of "lower-class culture" in well-liked boys, who seem not at all in rebellion against other persons or against such "middle-class" institutions as the school.

This picture of the differences in the operation of personality and cultural factors at different socioeconomic levels seems new.

Appendixes

Appendix A
Instructions and Materials

TEXAS CHRISTIAN UNIVERSITY — UNIVERSITY OF MINNESOTA
PEER RELATIONS STUDY

Instructions to the Teacher for Obtaining Peer Choices

Tell your students to put away all materials.

Pass out one special pencil, one card (blue cards to boys, pink cards to girls) and one name list to each student. (Make sure that boys receive boys' name lists and that girls receive girls' lists.)

If you have a student whose name does not appear on the appropriate lists, have your students enter that name on the lists, giving it the next consecutive number.

If you had a student who has dropped, have your students draw a line through that student's name and number on the name list only.

Read the following instructions to the class:

1. You have each received a name list (hold up the list), a card (hold up the card), and a special pencil (hold up the pencil).

2. Look at the name list. Find your own name on the list. Note the number just before your name. This is your number.

3. Now look at the card [Fig. 5]. The first two columns are labeled "Your Number."
   Suppose your number were 37. You would draw a heavy, straight line in the 3 box in the first column, and a heavy, straight line in the 7 box in the second column.
   Using your own number now, mark the first two columns in

183

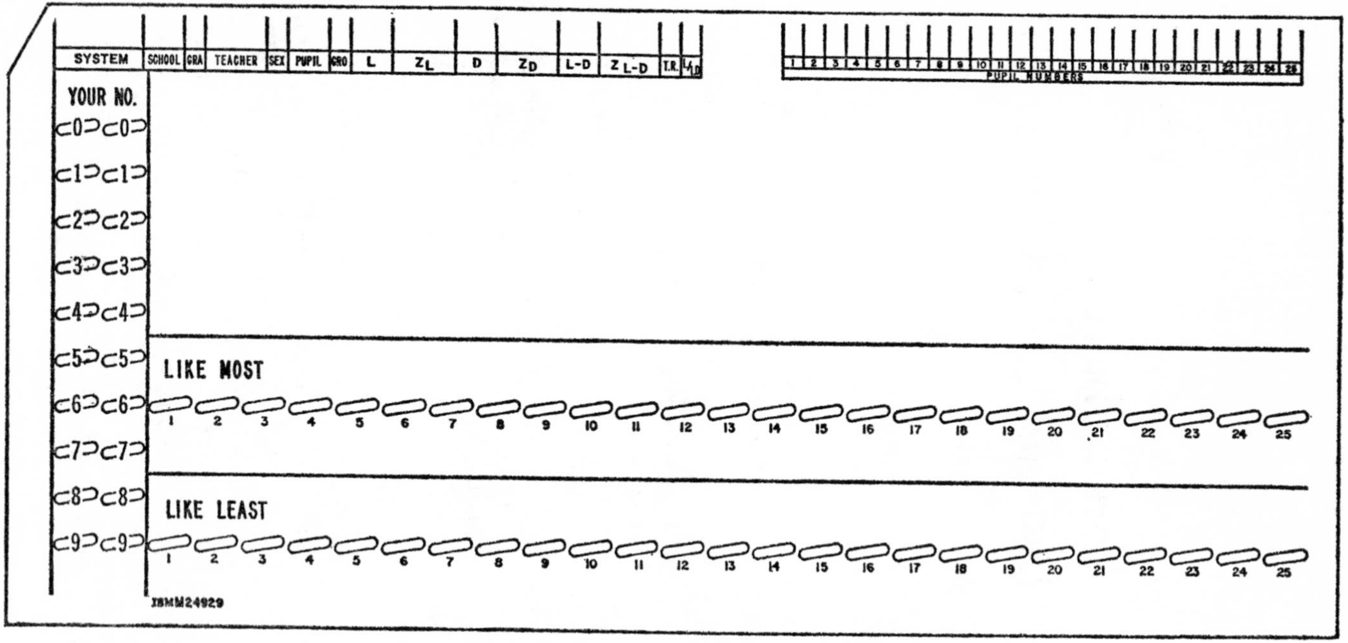

184

Figure 5. Peer nomination card — blue for boys, pink for girls.

that manner. Make the line heavy, and make it the length of the box. Do *not* let the line go outside the box. (Give time for all to do this correctly.)

4. Look again at the name list. Draw a circle around your name and number. This is to remind you that in the steps to follow you are not to use your own number.

5. Now think of the person on the list whom you like most. Find his or her number on the list.

6. Find this number on the card, in the long row labeled "Like Most." (Hold up the card and indicate the row to the students.)

7. Put a heavy, straight, long line in the box just above this number. (Give time for all to do this.)

8. Now do the same thing for the next three persons on the list whom you like very much. (Give time for all to do this.)

9. Do the same thing for the *two* persons on the list whom you like least, but this time mark in the long row labeled "Like Least."

10. Now look closely at the card. Make sure that you have marked your number correctly.

11. Make sure that you have marked exactly *four* boxes in the "Like Most" row.

12. Make sure that you have marked exactly *two* boxes in the "Like Least" row.

13. Make sure that there are no pencil marks anywhere else on the card except for "Your Number," and "Like Most" and "Like Least."

14. Turn the card over and write your name and your teacher's name on the back.

End of instructions to students.

Please take up all materials. Check the cards carefully to make sure that each student's identification number is correct, that he has marked the correct number of responses on the card, and that he has not marked a box for which there is no student in your class.

For each student who was absent during the administering of this scale, please mark-sense his or her number on an appropriately colored card. Include this card with the others.

Place the students' cards in the properly marked envelope. Place this envelope and all other materials (except the pencils) back in the large envelope.

Place the pencils in the specially marked container.

Follow the instructions given by your local coordinator for turning in all materials.

PEER RELATIONS AND PERSONALITY STUDY
TEACHERS' RATINGS INSTRUCTIONS

The Peer Relations Study is concerned with the relations of Peer Acceptance and Peer Rejection to personality development and adjustment. This phase of the research involves *teacher evaluation of pupil's peer relations*. Previous research has indicated that teachers' judgments of pupils' peer relations are generally one of the most valid sources of information. Please make your ratings carefully, following the instructions below.

Peer group acceptance and rejection are defined differently from adjustment. Children classified as *accepted* are those who have frequent, nonconflicting relations with other children. This may range from popularity and leadership to followership, even in low status roles. As long as a child is included in play groups and remains in communication with the others, he may be considered accepted to some degree.

Children who are disliked, ostracized, excluded, shunned, and kept outside of their peer group are classified as *rejected*. In some cases these children may show no signs of maladjustment. However, if they are rejected by their peers, they should be so classified.

Rating Categories. Your ratings are to be made on the Teacher Rating Cards [Fig. 6], which are *yellow* colored for boys and *green* colored for girls. In all other respects these cards are identical. Be careful to use the properly marked cards for these ratings. Each student is to be rated in one of the following seven categories which you think describes him or her best.

1. EXTREMELY HIGH — OUTSTANDING PEER RELATIONS. One of top boys (or girls) in class, an outstanding leader, best-liked child in class, by both girls and boys, best accepted by other children.

2. EXTREMELY HIGH — SUPERIOR PEER RELATIONS. One of the most popular members of class, a strong leader, highly accepted by other children, well liked by both boys and girls.

3. HIGH ACCEPTANCE AMONG PEERS. Liked by most of the other children, one of first chosen on playground, has many friends, accepted by most of the children.

4. MODERATE ACCEPTANCE AMONG PEERS. Chosen about the middle by other children, a follower, but others like him (her),

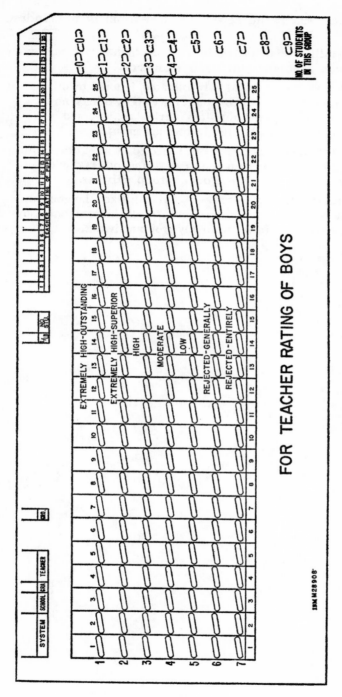

Figure 6. Teacher rating card — yellow for boys, green for girls.

generally accepted; liked, but not to a high extent, not overly popular, but other children think he's OK.

5. LOW PEER RELATIONS. Merely tolerated, ignored by others, but not rejected, accepted by some, rejected by others, no close friends; not rejected but often overlooked, accepted by younger children, but not by own age group.

6. REJECTED GENERALLY BY PEERS. Rejected by most other children, picked on, teased, blamed for everything, others don't want him on their side, pushed out of group activities.

7. REJECTED ENTIRELY BY PEERS. Actively disliked, laughed at, made a fool of, scapegoat, rejected by all children, both boys and girls, never included in any group activities.

Appendix B
Tables

Appendix Table 1. Mean Split-Half Reliability Coefficients for LM and LL Scores in Successive Years, by Sex and by State

Year and Sex	N		LM		LL	
	Minn.	Texas	Minn.	Texas	Minn.	Texas
Fifth Grade						
First year						
Boys	719	390	.65	.76	.75	.70
Girls	792	405	.67	.66	.73	.79
Second year						
Boys	804	449	.74	.75	.75	.70
Girls	747	434	.66	.67	.73	.73
Third year						
Boys	737	441	.56	.67	.69	.72
Girls	702	407	.56	.59	.69	.70
Sixth Grade						
First year						
Boys	1012	379	.61	.72	.75	.76
Girls	959	379	.60	.69	.73	.68
Second year						
Boys	841	406	.67	.66	.76	.73
Girls	901	424	.66	.57	.77	.72
Third year						
Boys	815	430	.65	.67	.74	.74
Girls	795	437	.62	.70	.79	.75

Appendix Table 2. Comparisons of Stability Coefficients by State and SES
Boys and Girls Combined

Interval between Tests, State, and SES	LM	LL	LM – LL	TR	(LM – LL)/TR
Minnesota vs. Texas					
One-year interval (grade 3 vs. 4)					
Texas[a]	.47	.39	.49	.42	.55
Minnesota[b]	.55	.36	.56	.49	.62
Two-year interval (grade 3 vs. 5)					
Texas[a]	.44	.34	.46	.38	.51
Minnesota[b]	.48	.35	.49	.48	.57
Three-year interval (grade 3 vs. 6)					
Texas[a]	.43	.34	.46	.41	.51
Minnesota[b]	.42	.33	.44	.45	.52
SES III *vs.* SES IV					
One-year interval (grade 3 vs. 4)					
SES III[c]	.60	.28[d]	.58	.52	.64
SES IV[e]	.47	.45	.54	.45	.61
Two-year interval (grade 3 vs. 5)					
SES III[c]	.50	.34	.51	.49	.58
SES IV[e]	.45	.36	.47	.46	.55
Three-year interval (grade 3 vs. 6)					
SES III[c]	.42	.33	.44	.49	.53
SES IV[e]	.41	.33	.44	.39	.52

[a]N = 486.   [b]N = 670.   [c]N = 388.
[d]Boys, .17; girls, .38.   [e]N = 282.

Appendix Table 3. Intraclass Correlations for Sets of Non-Twin Siblings on Five
Measures of Peer Acceptance-Rejection, Two States Combined

Sets of Siblings	No. of Sets	LM	LL	LM – LL	TR	2(LM – LL)/TR
Sets of two						
Boy, boy	1,114	.29	.18	.32	.26	.37
Girl, girl	1,026	.29	.21	.30	.22	.35
Boy, girl	2,133	.19	.20	.24	.22	.29
Total	4,273	.25	.20	.27	.27	.32
Sets of three						
Boy, boy, boy	89	.30	.14	.24	.22	.28
Girl, girl, girl	97	.33	.13	.31	.30	.38
Boy, boy, girl	233	.27	.24	.32	.21	.34
Girl, girl, boy	231	.30	.16	.31	.22	.34
Total	650	.28	.19	.29	.22	.32

Appendix Table 4. Intraclass Correlations for Pairs of Twins and Other Siblings, Both States and Both Sexes Combined

Pairs	LM	LL	LM – LL	TR	2(LM – LL)/TR
Like sex					
Identical twins (74 pr)	.62	.65	.70	.72	.77
Fraternal twins (78 pr)	.41	.47	.52	.41	.53
Non-twin siblings (2,140 pr)	.29	.20	.31	.24	.36
Unlike sex					
Fraternal twins (85 pr)	.24	.26	.27	.11	.24
Non-twin siblings (2,133 pr)	.19	.20	.24	.22	.29

Appendix Table 5. Intraclass Correlations for Pairs of Twins and Other Siblings by Sex, Both States Combined

Pairs and Sex	LM	LL	LM – LL	TR	2(LM – LL)/TR
Separated by Sex					
Identical twins					
Boy/boy (33 pr)	.72	.54	.68	.78	.80
Girl/girl (41 pr)	.55	.71	.72	.68	.74
Fraternal twins					
Boy/boy (47 pr)	.34	.44	.50	.44	.56
Girl/girl (31 pr)	.52	.54	.56	.36	.53
Boy/girl (85 pr)	.24	.26	.27	.11	.24
Both Sexes Combined					
Identical twins					
Minnesota (33 pr)	.76	.75	.84	.77	.87
Texas (41 pr)	.51	.49	.55	.66	.62
Fraternal twins					
Like sex, Minnesota (38 pr)	.35	.63	.55	.34	.47
Like sex, Texas (40 pr) ...	.47	.26	.49	.45	.56
Unlike sex, Minnesota (41 pr)	.25	.43	.35	.11	.28
Unlike sex, Texas (44 pr)..	.20	.03	.15	.13	.17
Set of two					
Like sex, Minnesota (1,432 pr)	.28	.17	.29	.24	.36
Like sex, Texas (708 pr) ..	.34	.24	.36	.26	.40
Unlike sex, Minnesota (1,419 pr)	.14	.17	.20	.18	.25
Unlike sex, Texas (714 pr)..	.28	.24	.33	.28	.37

Appendix Table 6. Frequency Distributions of Item Responses on the Family History Questionnaire for High- and Low-Choice Children

Item	Low Choice Ss (N = 25)	High Choice Ss (N = 34)
Parents' health		
Either parent	12	9
Child's medical history	9	4
Social history of the family		
Death of family member	4	8
Separation or divorce	6	4
Psychiatric history of "need for psychiatric examination: family member other than child"	9	2
Welfare history	11	2
Criminal history		
Parent	6	1
Child	9	1
Other family characteristics		
Family mobility	6	0
Occupational history	12	2
Father graduated from high school	4	19
Mother graduated from high school	3	19

References

References

Almack, J. C. The influence of intelligence on the selection of associates. *School and Society*, 1922, 16, 529–530.

Ames, R. G., & Higgins, A. C. Note of a UNIVAC program for contingency analysis in the large scale sociogram. *Sociometry*, 1963, 26, 128.

Anderson, W. F. Relation of Lorge-Thorndike Intelligence Test scores of public school pupils to the socioeconomic status of their parents. *Journal of Experimental Education*, 1962, 31, 73–76.

Ausubel, D. P. Reciprocity and assumed reciprocity of acceptance among adolescents. *Sociometry*, 1953, 16, 339–448.

——. Sociempathy as a function of sociometric status in an adolescent group. *Human Relations*, 1955, 8, 75–84.

—— & Schiff, H. M. Some intrapersonal and interpersonal determinants of individual differences in sociempathic ability among adolescents. *Journal of Social Psychology*, 1955, 41, 39–56.

Bell, G. B., & Hall, H. E., Jr. The relationship between leadership and empathy. *Journal of Abnormal and Social Psychology*, 1954, 49, 156–157.

Bonney, M. E. A study of social status on the second grade level. *Journal of Genetic Psychology*, 1942, 60, 271–305.

——. The constancy of sociometric scores and their relationship to teacher judgments of social success and to personality self-ratings. *Sociometry*, 1943, 6, 409–424. (a)

——. The relative stability of social, intellectual, and academic status in grades II to IV, and the interrelationships between these various forms of growth. *Journal of Educational Psychology*, 1943, 34, 88–102. (b)

——. Relationship between social success, family size, socioeconomic home background and intelligence. *Sociometry*, 1944, 7, 26–37.

——. A sociometric study of the relationship of some factors to mutual friendships on the elementary, secondary, and college levels. *Sociometry*, 1946, 9, 21–47.

Bordua, D. J. (Ed.) *Sociological theories and their implications for juvenile delinquency: A report of a children's bureau conference.* Washington, D.C.: U.S. Department of Health, Education, and Welfare, Social Security Administration, Children's Bureau, 1960.

Bower, E. M. *Early identification of emotionally handicapped children in school.* Springfield, Ill.: Thomas, 1960.

Cattell, R. B. Teacher's personality descriptions of six-year-olds: A check on structure. *British Journal of Educational Psychology*, 1963, 33, 219–235.

Chowdhry, K., & Newcomb, T. M. The relative abilities of leaders and non-leaders to estimate opinions of their own groups. *Journal of Abnormal and Social Psychology*, 1952, 47, 51–57.

Cohen, A. K. *Delinquent boys: The culture of the gang.* Glencoe, Ill.: Free Press, 1955.

Cohn, T. S., Fisher, A., & Brown, V. Leadership and predicting attitudes of others. *Journal of Social Psychology*, 1961, 55, 199–206.

Conger, J. J., & Miller, W. C. *Personality, social class, and delinquency.* New York: Wiley, 1966.

Cox, S. H. Family background effects on personality development and social acceptance. Ph.D. thesis, Texas Christian University, 1966.

Criswell, J. H. A sociometric study of race cleavage in the classroom. *Archives of Psychology*, 1939, No. 235.

Dahlke, H. O. Determinants of sociometric relations among children in the elementary school. *Sociometry*, 1953, 16, 327–338.

Davis, J. A. Correlates of sociometric status among peers. *Journal of Educational Research*, 1957, 50, 561–569.

Elkins, D. Some factors related to the choice status of 90 eighth grade children in a school society. *Genetic Psychology Monographs*, 1958, 58, 207–272.

Exline, R. V. Interrelations among two dimensions of sociometric status, group congeniality and accuracy of social perception. *Sociometry*, 1960, 23, 85–101.

Festinger, L. The analysis of sociograms using matrix algebra. *Human Relations*, 1949, 2, 153–158.

Forsyth, E., & Katz, L. A matrix approach to the analysis of sociometric data. *Sociometry*, 1946, 9, 340–347.

Gage, N. L. Judging interests from expressive behavior. *Psychological Monographs*, 1952, 66, No. 18 (Whole No. 350).

_____, Leavitt, G. S., & Stone, G. C. Teachers' understanding of their pupils and pupils' rating of their teachers. *Psychological Monographs*, 1955, 69 (21, Whole No. 406).

Gallagher, J. J. Social status of children related to intelligence, propinquity and social perception. *Elementary School Journal*, 1958, 58, 225–231.

_____ & Crowder, T. The adjustment of gifted children in the regular classroom. *Exceptional Children*, 1956, 23, 306–312, 317–319.

Galton, F. *English men of science: Their nature and nurture.* London: Macmillan, 1874.

Glanzer, M., & Glaser, R. Techniques for the study of group structure and behavior: I. Analysis of structure. *Psychological Bulletin*, 1959, 56, 317–332.

Goslin, D. A. Accuracy of self-perception and social acceptance. *Sociometry*, 1962, 25, 283–296.

Green, G. H. Insight and group adjustment. *Journal of Abnormal and Social Psychology*, 1948, 43, 49–61.

Greer, F. L., Galanter, E. G., & Nordlie, P. G. Interpersonal knowledge and individual and group effectiveness. *Journal of Abnormal and Social Psychology*, 1954, 49, 411–414.

Gronlund, N. E. The accuracy of teachers' judgments concerning the sociometric status of sixth grade pupils. *Sociometry*, 1950, 13, 197–225. (a)

_____. The accuracy of teachers' judgment concerning the sociometric status of sixth grade pupils. *Sociometry*, 1950, 13, 329–357. (b)

_____. The relative ability of home-room teachers and special-subject teachers to judge the social acceptability of pre-adolescent pupils. *Journal of Educational Research*, 1954, 48, 381–391.

_____. Sociometric status and sociometric perception. *Sociometry,* 1955, 18, 122–127.

_____. *Sociometry in the classroom.* New York: Harper, 1959.

_____ & Algard, P. W. The relation between teachers' judgments of pupils' sociometric status and intelligence. *Elementary School Journal,* 1958, 264–268.

Grossman, B., & Wrighter, J. The relationship between selection-rejection and intelligence, social status, and personality amongst sixth-grade children. *Sociometry,* 1948, 11, 346–355.

Guinouard, D. E., & Rychlak, J. F. Personality correlates of sociometric popularity in elementary school children. *Personnel and Guidance Journal,* 1962, 40, 438–442.

Hardy, M. C. Social recognition at the elementary school age. *Journal of Social Psychology,* 1937, 8, 365–384.

Hathaway, S. R., & Monachesi, E. D. *Analyzing and predicting juvenile delinquency with the MMPI.* Minneapolis: University of Minnesota Press, 1953.

Hites, R. W., & Campbell, D. T. A test of the ability of fraternity leaders to estimate group opinion. *Journal of Social Psychology,* 1950, 32, 95–100.

Jablon, S., Neel, J. V., Gershowitz, H., & Atkinson, G. F. The NAS-NRC twin panel: Methods of construction of the panel, zygosity diagnosis, and proposed use. *American Journal of Human Genetics,* 1967, 19, No. 2, 136–161.

Jamrich, J. X. Application of matrices in the analysis of sociometric data. *Journal of Experimental Education,* 1960, 28, 249–252.

Jenkins, R. L. The psychopathic delinquent. In *Social work in the current scene: Selected papers,* 76th Annual Meeting, National Conference of Social Work, June 12–17, 1949. New York: Columbia University Press, 1950.

Jennings, H. *Leadership and isolation.* New York: Longmans, 1943.

Johnson, G. O. A study of the social position of mentally handicapped children in the regular grades. *American Journal of Mental Deficiency,* 1950, 55, 60–89.

Jones, H. Order of birth. In C. Murchison (Ed.), *A handbook of child psychology.* (2nd ed.) Worcester, Mass.: Clark University Press, 1933. Pp. 551–589.

Justman, J., & Wrightstone, J. A comparison of three methods of measuring pupil status in the classroom. *Educational and Psychological Measurement,* 1951, 11, 362–367.

Katz, L. On the matrix analysis of sociometric data. *Sociometry,* 1947, 10, 233–241.

_____. A new status index derived from sociometric analysis. *Psychometrika,* 1953, 18, 39–43.

Kogan, N., & Tagiuri, R. On the visibility of choice and awareness of being chosen. *Psychological Reports,* 1958, 4, 83–86.

Kvaraceus, W. C., & Miller, W. B. *Delinquent Behavior.* Washington, D.C.: National Education Association, 1959. Pp. 32–41.

Lewis, M. N., & Spilka, B. Sociometric choice status, empathy, assimilative and disowning projection. *Psychological Record,* 1960, 10, 95–100.

Loehlin, J. C. A heredity-environment analysis of personality inventory data. In S. G. Vandenberg (Ed.), *Methods and goals in human behavior genetics.* New York: Academic Press, 1965.

Loomis, C. P. Ethnic cleavages in the Southwest as reflected in two high schools. *Sociometry,* 6, 1943, 7–25.

Luce, R. D., & Perry, A. D. A method of matrix analysis of group structure. *Psychometrika,* 1949, 14, 95–116.

McGahan, F. E. Factors associated with leadership ability of the elementary school child. M.A. thesis, North Texas State Teachers College, 1940.

McNemar, Q. *The revision of the Stanford-Binet Scale.* New York: Houghton Mifflin, 1942.

_____. *Psychological statistics.* New York: Wiley, 1962.

Maller, J. B. Cooperation and competition — an experimental study in motivation. *Teachers College Contributions to Education*, 1929, No. 384.

Mitchell, A. Some statistics of idiocy. *Edinburgh Medical Journal*, 1866, 11, pt. 2, 639–645.

Moreno, J. L. *Who shall survive?* Washington, D.C.: Nervous and Mental Disease Publishing Co., 1934.

Mouton, J. S., Blake, R. R., & Fruchter, B. The reliability of sociometric measure. *Sociometry*, 1955, 18, 7–48.

Murphy, G., Murphy, L. B., & Newcomb, T. M. *Experimental social psychology*. (Rev. ed.) New York: Harper, 1937.

Neugarten, B. Social class and friendship among school children. *American Journal of Sociology*, 1946, 51, 305–313.

Neumeyer, M. H. *Juvenile delinquency in modern society*. (3rd ed.) Princeton, N.J.: Van Nostrand, 1961. Ch. 11.

O'Connor, W. F. The interrelationships of social perception, sociometric status, personality and the ability to judge personality traits. School of Aviation medicine, USN, Rep. No. MR 005 13-5001, Sub. 2, No. 9, iii, 1960.

Piers, E. V., & Harris, D. B. Age and other correlates of self-concept in children. *Journal of Educational Psychology*, 1963, 55, 91–95.

Porterfield, O. V., & Schlichting, H. F. Peer status and reading achievement. *Journal of Educational Research*, 1961, 54, 291–297.

Proctor, C. H., & Loomis, C. P. An analysis of sociometric data. In M. Jahoda, M. Deutsch, & S. W. Cook (Eds.), *Research methods in social relations: With special reference to prejudice*, pt. 2. New York: Dryden, 1951. Pp. 561–585.

Remmers, H. H., & Bauernfeind, R. H. *Manual for the SRA Junior Inventory Form S*. Chicago: Science Research Associates, 1957.

Roe, A., & Siegelman, M. A parent-child relations questionnaire. *Child Development*, 1963, 34, 355–369.

Roff, M. A factorial study of the Fels Parent Behavior Scales. *Child Development*, 1949, 20, 29–45.

_____. Intra-family resemblances in personality characteristics. *Journal of Psychology*, 1950, 30, 199–227.

_____. Preservice personality problems and subsequent adjustment to military service: Gross outcome in relation to acceptance-rejection at induction and military service. School of Aviation Medicine, USAF, Rep. No. 55-138, 1956.

_____. Preservice personality problems and subsequent adjustment to military service: The prediction of psychoneurotic reactions. School of Aviation Medicine, USAF, Rep. No. 57-136, 1957.

_____. Preservice personality problems and subsequent adjustments to military service: A replication of "The prediction of psychoneurotic reactions." School of Aviation Medicine, USAF, Rep. No. 58-151, 1959.

_____. Relations between certain preservice factors and psychoneurosis during military duty. *Armed Forces Medical Journal*, 1960, 11, 152–160.

_____. Childhood social interactions and young adult bad conduct. *Journal of Abnormal and Social Psychology*, 1961, 63, 33–337. (a)

_____. The service-related experience of a sample of juvenile delinquents. U.S. Army Medical Research and Development Command, Rep. No. 61-1, January 1961. (b)

_____. Childhood social interaction and young adult psychosis. *Journal of Clinical Psychology*, 1963, 19, 152–157. (a)

_____. The service-related experience of a sample of juvenile delinquents. II. A replication on a larger sample in another state. U.S. Army Medical Research and Development Command, Rep. No. 63-2, December 1963. (b)

———. The service-related experience of a sample of juvenile delinquents. III. The predictive significance of juvenile confinement. U.S. Army Medical Research and Development Command, Rep. No. 64-3, March 1964.

———. Some developmental aspects of schizoid personality. U.S. Army Medical Research and Development Command, Rep. No. 65-4, March 1965.

———. Some childhood and adolescent characteristics of adult homosexuals. U.S. Army Medical Research and Development Command, Rep. No. 66-5, May 1966.

———. The service-related experience of a sample of juvenile delinquents. IV. Results with a second Minnesota sample. U.S. Army Medical Research and Development Command, Rep. No. 67-6, March 1967.

———. The service-related experience of a sample of juvenile delinquents. V. The relation between education, number of juvenile apprehensions, and outcome in service. U.S. Army Medical Research and Development Command, Rep. No. 68-7, May 1968.

———. The service-related experience of juvenile delinquents. VI. The predictive value of education in a second delinquent sample and in a normal control group. U.S. Army Medical Research and Development Command, Rep. No. 69-8, April 1969.

———. Juvenile delinquency and military service. In R. W. Little (Ed.), *Selective Service and American society*. New York: Russell Sage Foundation, 1969.

———. Some life history factors in relation to various types of adult maladjustment. In M. Roff & D. F. Ricks (Eds.), *Life history research in psychopathology*. Vol. 1. Minneapolis: University of Minnesota Press, 1970. Pp. 265–287.

———. A two-factor approach to juvenile delinquency and the later histories of juvenile delinquents. In M. Roff, L. N. Robins, & M. Pollack (Eds.), *Life history research in psychopathology*. Vol. 2. Minneapolis: University of Minnesota Press, 1972. Pp. 77–101.

———, Mink, W., & Hinrichs, G. *Developmental abnormal psychology*. New York: Holt, 1966.

Roff, M., & Ricks, D. F. (Eds.), *Life history research in psychopathology*. Vol. 1. Minneapolis: University of Minnesota Press, 1970.

Roff, M., Robins, L. N., & Pollack, M. (Eds.), *Life history research in psychopathology*. Vol. 2. Minneapolis: University of Minnesota Press, 1972.

Roff, M., & Sells, S. B. Relations between intelligence and sociometric status in groups differing in sex and socioeconomic background. *Psychological Reports*, 1965, 16, 511–516.

———. The relations between the status of chooser and chosen in a sociometric situation at the grade school level. *Psychology in the Schools*, 1967, 4, 101–111.

———. Juvenile delinquency in relation to peer acceptance-rejection and socioeconomic status. *Psychology in the Schools*, 1968, 5, 3–18.

Satterlee, R. L. Sociometric analysis and personality adjustment. *California Journal of Educational Research*, 1955, 6, 181–184.

Sells, S. B., & Roff, M. Peer acceptance-rejection and birth order. *Psychology in the Schools*, 1964, 1, 156–162. (a)

———. Problems in the estimation of peer rejection in the early grades. *Psychology in the Schools*, 1964, 1, 256–262. (b)

———. Family influence as reflected in peer acceptance-rejection resemblance of siblings as compared with random sets of school children. *Psychology in the Schools*, 1965, 2, 133–137.

———. Peer acceptance-rejection and personality development. Office of Education, U.S. Department of Health, Education, and Welfare, Final Report, Project No. OE 5-0417. January 1967.

Sewell, W. H., & Haller, A. O. Factors in the relationship between social status and the personality adjustment of the child. *American Sociological Review*, 1959, 24, 511–520.

Short, J. F., & Strodtbeck, F. L. *Group process and gang delinquency.* Chicago: University of Chicago Press, 1965.

Sullivan, E. T., Clark, W. W., & Tiegs, E. W. *Manual of the California Test of Mental Maturity.* Los Angeles: California Test Bureau, 1957.

Taguiri, R., Kogan, N., & Long, L. M. K. Differentiation of sociometric choice and status relations in a group. *Psychological Reports*, 1958, 4, 523–526.

Terman, L. H. A preliminary study in the psychology and pedagogy of leadership. *Pedagogical Seminary*, 1904, 9, 413–451.

Trent, R. D. Anxiety and accuracy of perception of sociometric status among institutionalized delinquent boys. *Journal of Genetic Psychology*, 1959, 94, 85–91.

Ullmann, C. A. Teachers, peers and tests as predictors of adjustment. *Journal of Educational Psychology*, 1957, 48, 257–267.

Winer, B. J. *Statistical principles in experimental design.* New York: McGraw-Hill, 1962.

Wirt, R. D., & Briggs, P. F. Personality and environmental factors in the development of delinquency. *Psychological Monographs*, 1959, 73, No. 15 (Whole No. 485).

Young, L. L., & Cooper, D. H. Some factors associated with popularity. *Journal of Educational Psychology*, 1944, 35, 513–535.

Index

Index

attitudes, 137, 139, 140; and peer status, 140

Middle-choice children: common traits of, 41, 44. *See also* Illustrative cases

Minnesota Multiphasic Personality Inventory (MMPI): used in studies of delinquency, 171

Mobility of family, *see* Family adjustment

Moreno, J. L.: peer choice and racial background, 94

Murphy, G., Murphy, L. B., Newcomb, T. M.: influences of birth order, 91

Negative peer ratings: reasons for inclusion, 14; meaning of, 57

Open-end questionnaire, 110, 120–124, 178. *See also* Family information

Overt concern of parents: 130, 136, 145; and child's IQ, self-concept, 139; and child's medical history, 139; correlated with other parental attitudes, 143–144; and peer status, 138; and social level, 129. *See also* Parental attitudes

Parental attitudes: 127, 128, 145; and characteristics of child, 139; consistency, effect on child's personality development, 9, 134, 145–146; and peer status, 128; Roe-Siegelman ratings, 129–130, 136, 142–144. *See also* Casual-demanding parental attitudes; Loving-rejecting parental attitudes; Overt concern of parents

Parents' self-rating: correlation with child's rating of parents, 143; correlation with peer status, 179

Peer acceptance-rejection, *see* Peer status

Peer status: measures, Like Most (LM), Like Least (LL) and LM − LL, 6, 11–15, 57, 172–173

— scores: combined with teacher rating scores, 14, 59; correlations with teacher ratings, 12, 58, 59, 66–72, 175; intercorrelations by sex, grade, state, 57–58; Minnesota and Texas distributions of, 21–22; by SES, 8, 57–58, 60; stability coefficients, 61–66, 174–175. *See also* Chooser-chosen correlations; Matrices

— related factors: adult maladjustment, 9, 19; birth order, 8, 91–93, 177; delinquency, 151–154, 168; family characteristics, 19, 112–119, 123–124, 178;

father's employment history, 124; intelligence, 7, 86–90; parents' self-ratings, 179; racial or ethnic background, 8, 94–98; and SES, 86–90. *See also* High-choice children; Illustrative cases; Low-choice children; Middle-choice children

Porterfield, O. V.: achievement scores and social acceptability, 88

Pretesting, 13, 14

Psychiatric history of family, *see* Family adjustment

Racial or ethnic background: and delinquency, 165–167; and peer status, 8, 94, 95. *See also* Spanish surname children

Rating dimensions: of peer status, 13, 14

Roe-Siegelman scales, 130, 143, 179. *See also* Parental attitudes

Schlichting, H. F.: achievement scores and social acceptability, 88

Self-concept: and child's perception of parents' behavior, 137; and parental attitudes, 139

Self-concept questionnaire, 130, 139–140, 179

Self-rating instruments: compared with other scoring procedures, 11, 28; self-concept questionnaire, 130, 139–140; SRA Junior Inventory, 140

Sibling peer status correlations, *see* Twin and sibling peer status resemblance

Sims Social Class Identification Scale: as basis for SES, 18

Social perception: interpersonal, 7, 73–75, 76–81; previous studies involving, 74. *See also* Chooser-chosen correlations

Socioeconomic status (SES): classification of schools by, 18; determination of, 18–25, 120; effect of student's on teacher rating accuracy, 68–69, 71; and intelligence, 134, 137, 146, 176–177; and parental attitudes, 134, 139; and peer status, 86–90; and racial background, 165; and stability coefficients, 66. *See also* Family information; Illustrative cases; Intelligence; Peer status; Teacher ratings

Spanish surname children: 94–109; and control pupils, peer status and teacher